COMING HOME

Also by Shepard Ginandes, M.D.

THE SCHOOL WE HAVE

Coming Home

*How parents and grown children
can confront each other more openly,
communicate more freely,
and become friends*

Shepard Ginandes, M.D.

A Merloyd Lawrence Book
Delacorte Press / Seymour Lawrence

Library of Congress Cataloging in Publication Data

Ginandes, Shepard, 1928-
Coming home.

"A Merloyd Lawrence book."
1. Young adults—United States. 2. Parent and child.
3. Interpersonal communication. 4. Conflict of generations. I. Title.
HQ799.7.G56   301.42'7   76-8866
ISBN 0-440-01447-6

This book is dedicated
to those young adults and their parents
who were honest and courageous enough
to confront each other until they
became friends—and to make
me aware of the process.
Their stories became
this book.

SPECIAL THANKS

Special thanks to Lisa Dennen,
my researcher-interviewer, for her skill
and humanness, drawing honesty and real reactions
from some of the people you will read about.
My deepest gratitude also to
the staff and students of The School We Have,
the laboratory in which I learned about
the struggle this book is about.

Contents

Introduction

Any psychiatrist is well aware that all of us settle issues with our parents within our own minds. Our parents gave us life, our genes—our DNA. They were also our gods. All sense of what human contact feels like, what basic trust can be, comes from our mothers and fathers. Our earliest notions of good and evil, of feeling like a nice or naughty child, were trained into us by them. We got our Ten Commandments from them, all of us, without having to climb Mount Sinai. And further, our deepest decisions about whether we want to be man or woman, whether we accept or resist the gender we were born into, come from our childhood observation of how our parents accepted and dealt with theirs. Our first romances were with them; the ways we love and work—our sense of being basically worthwhile or worthless—came from our interaction with them. All this and more. So when we reach the fork in the road and leave home, we take with us the personality that was forged in their workshop.

This self we bring into the first years of living on our own. And all too soon we begin to find out whether this parent-crafted self makes it in the world of here and now. Obviously, the world we live in at age twenty-one has changed from the world of ten to twenty years ago when we were children. And it is even more different from the world of twenty years before that when our parents were children and getting basic training from *their* parents. You might say that the values and policies governing the upbringing of a child from 1953–65 are those his or her parents incorporated from *their* parents in 1930–42, as modified by the parents' own young adult years, say 1950–60. And since that time things have changed *much more* rapidly, even exponentially, I'm tempted to believe: pot, widespread drug addiction, LSD trips, the "youth culture," hippies, the Symbionese Liberation Army, the labor committees, peace marches, Watergate and Vietnam, communes, group marriages, unisex and gay liberation, even the worship of "social change." The self that now goes into the world at age twenty-one is going to need some revisions in order to stay afloat in the sea of conflicting values and goals. Young people must ask: Should I marry and have children despite divorces, pollution, ecological catastrophes and ICBMs? Should I invest my trust fund in falling blue-chip stocks or cash it in and go to Katmandu? Should I do Tantric Yoga or the Royal Canadian Air Force exercises? Meditate or get stoned or booze it up like Dad? Study Zen or computer technology? In the face of this sort of decision, many parents are not of much help. Young adults must make these decisions *themselves*. The task is more difficult now that the old cultural systems of rewards and restraints for the young are losing their effectiveness.

Upon the foundation of the families they came from and the selves they bring with them from home, in an environment of accelerating and bewildering change, young adults must modify their child selves into viable adult selves. Erik Erikson saw this as the major task of adolescence—a formative stage of human development—the formation of an identity that feels right, that expresses who a person is, that uses his or her endowments and talents, that embodies his or her cultural background, and that fits into the world *here and now*.

Much has been written about adolescence and how identity formation proceeds. We can read about the problems and vicissitudes of the growing identity sense. Those of us who admire Erikson's work use his concepts daily in our clinical work with adolescents and give thanks for the clarity of his thinking and perception.

But I have heard a further theme in the lives of the young adults I know. This theme is a yearning, a sense of business unfinished. Not only inside the self, but also between the young adult child and his older parents. Many of these young people, now no longer living at home, who are struggling to find expression for who they are and what they want to do in life, have told me about a need they feel to make a new kind of relationship with their parents. No longer as a product of the parents' homes, but as a *person* relating to a *person*—"Can we accept each other as *people;* can we like each other? Can we be friends?" In order for this to happen, old battles must be fought through and hatchets buried. Many of these young people have gone bravely back to their parents, intent upon getting closer *as equals.* Sometimes this happens easily, when all parties feel basically good about the parent-child times. Sometimes the process is agonizing, when old deep grudges and wounds must be reprobed before they can heal. This book is the story of that campaign. The experiences it describes have convinced me that getting it together with one's parents, reconnecting the cultural discontinuity created by the breakaway at the end of adolescence, is a genuine part of the stage of our development called becoming an adult. Here are some of the stories I have heard, letters I have read, interviews I have arranged, firsthand reports from the front in the campaign to get back together, parents and child, as *people.*

In my first book, *The School We Have,* I explored some of the issues that split adolescents off from the values and beliefs of their parents in our society, that make some of our best young people become secret or overt rebels against the culture that feeds them. Together with some creative artists and crafts people and inspired therapists, I had put together a school where young people could evaluate themselves as individuals apart from the homes they grew up in. Here adolescents and young adults could find out who they are in new contexts—creative artwork and human problem-solving. Consolidated as independent people, they could then leave home and be functional people in the big world.

But this school, known as The School We Have, did more than expected. It became a small society with values of its own. It became an extended family not only for the young students, but also for its adult staff. Our staff members, already involved in their work as artists, craftspeople and therapists, progressed further toward self-actualization thanks to the school—just as far as the students did. I learned this because it also happened to me. Here I had created a "therapy scene," and it helped me grow as much as it did those who could be called "patients." I began to see that the school was functioning like a tribe—we all belong to it, we are all human participants in it. We put in what we can, it gives us what it can. Such a group, in Margaret Mead's expression, is a small "cocognitive" society, where we learn from each other regardless of age and status. Someday I hope to write about The School We Have as a small society dedicated to social change, in the direction of identity formation and self-actualization for all its members.

Another unexpected bonus has come from this school. It is a marvelous setting for research about the lives and feelings of adolescents and young adults. It was at the school, from its young students, that I began to hear about the issues that became the subject of this book. As the school got older, so did many of its students. And many of them, to my surprise, turned back toward home after becoming free from home. They wanted to go back and encounter their parents as equal people, to see if they could respect and like each other. In my private psychiatric practice and at The School We Have, I was privileged to watch and assist with this process. I have come to feel that coming home again is a normal part of human development—strengthening if it works, and potentially weakening if it fails. This book tells the story.

PART ONE

The need for honest confrontation

CHAPTER 1

Notes from your Barbie doll

Sally is away at college, in her freshman year. When she lived at home, she felt more and more that communication between her parents and herself was becoming empty and stereotyped, that she and her parents were not being honest about how they felt about each other. Bringing up this question brought no results; Sally's parents reacted first with surprise that Sally felt there was any barrier between them, and later denied they had any concealed feelings. That ended that. But Sally's frustrated feeling and desire to get closer to them did not go away.

When she was away at school, Sally decided she might be able to start a correspondence with her parents in which she would try to set an example, be totally frank about her feelings and encourage her parents to do the same. She began by referring to a couple of incidents that had arisen, the way her father had piled away her belongings in a closet, and an argument she had with him about her friends. Here are some of the highlights of that correspondence:

Dear Daddy,

What can I say to someone who says I have miserable taste in friends, when what he means is I don't have HIS taste in friends? Who piles away my things so roughly that they are ripped and crushed, and says he did it because they were "on the floor"? I don't think even YOU *believe that excuse—you even applied it to my rug. How can I accept such blatant lack of respect in the way you treat me? Then I wonder why I can't respect* MYSELF *now—I can't even show anger when people walk all over me. I've got so much work to do straightening out my own head before I even see myself as someone worthy of any respect.*

You don't like ME. *You don't do things for* ME. *You do them for* YOU. *I'm not a person you want to help—I'm a Barbie doll you buy accessories for, whatever you want her to have.* YOU *always wanted me to do chemistry with you when I was little—I did it out of a sense of guilt; you'd be lonely if I didn't do things with you. I was bored, but I felt pressure to pretend I was interested.* YOU *wanted me to ski with you. I did that too out of guilt. I've been your "little girl" before I was ever a person.* YOU *get something when you "give" me something. You get to be the father of an educated, talented, intelligent child. Maybe you feel pressure from your friends and people you work with to be able to be that kind of parent.*

What if I was a prostitute or a political prisoner, and you were sitting there in the living room with Alfred and Julie over cocktails, and Alfred said, "By the way, what's your daughter doing these days?" To you kids are your property, your investment. Your kids are a mirror in which you see what YOU *are.*

Daddy, if you did something I wanted, it was because our interests just happened to coincide. In a conflict, YOUR *interests won. You'd never have given me money for my Europe trip if you knew I would spend it in the ways I thought best.*

You don't like me, you don't even SEE *me. Even the pottery on my shelf you swept into the pile in the closet. Little pieces of what I really am—you don't want to see them.*

"I will help you only if you do what I think you should." —that is the essence of what you say. Even if your de-

cisions for me were better, job-wise, you should still leave decisions about me to me, and be willing to support me equally in whatever I decide. When I say "support," I include the emotional and financial. In our case, financial support is the most I can hope for unless you change. Financial support has been your only way of demonstrating emotional support. I can't imagine what other kind of emotional support could come from a person who has so little respect for me, to the point of showing no concern for my possessions, saying, "You can go roll with the pigs!"

Three weeks went by with no reply from Sally's father. Then her mother wrote:

Sally dear,

Daddy has spent days trying to write an answer to you. He's having a hard time communicating his deep feeling of love for you and telling also of his puzzlements, personal frustrations, shortcomings, etc. What he's trying to tell you is that he's not a perfect parent, but he cares for you and always will. He was glad you got your feelings out in the open and didn't keep them inside where they might hurt you. The yesterdays that haunted you will disappear now as you pour them out and get rid of them. All of us are sorry now for any unkind deed and we are wiser and more loving now. Love is the only thing that matters. The yesterdays are past. But a hopeful Sally who looks forward to her tomorrow in the faith that she will meet it with belief in her true values can be trusted to make a new meaningful day for everyone around her. We believe in you! The real you—kind, considerate, radiant, lovely, friendly and full of good humor. Every good thing you want you shall have. It is your divine right.

We will smile again when Sally does! Till then, we will also try to run away from her awful todays, albeit they still remain with us. We are sad—you can make us glad!

Sally replied:

Mother,

Don't write for Daddy. I can't trust your paraphrasing of his feelings. Besides, when you write for him it makes his lack of reply seem less conspicuous. I haven't asked for your *comments on* his *letters. Don't write for* BOTH *of you as if you* BOTH *were of one mind. It's confusing and impossible for me to deal with. You didn't mention the word "I" once in your letter. It was either "he feels" or "we feel." If you were going to write "we" (as if your positions separately aren't complicated enough without trying to consolidate them), then I'd expect to see both your signatures at the end of the letter. I think you say "we" and "he" because it scares you to be without his support when you express anything. Like when you say "all of us," meaning "all* TWO *of us!"*

That's just one of the word games you use so that you YOURSELF *avoid saying anything. The rest of your letter seemed to be an attempt to say things that would sound nice to me. It was either nice words whose meaning was vague at best, or just plain false. As I read it, I was stupefied by the* BULLSHIT *in every single sentence.*

"The yesterdays that haunted you" is no way of describing what I complain of. It makes the offense seem impersonal, and it implies that it isn't STILL HAPPENING. *"Older and wiser"—a cliché; you don't say what you mean by it. I don't care whether you're older and wiser, anyway. I just want to be treated like a person instead of an image.*

"The yesterdays are past . . . Love is the only thing that matters." A couple of high-sounding phrases to convince me that your point, whatever it is, is backed up by all kinds of humanistic wisdom.

"But a hopeful Sally . . . can be trusted to make a new meaningful day *for everyone around her"—What little meaning I can extract from that sentence is just* plain false. *If that's why you "trust" me, forget it. That sentence is just loaded with your expectations for the kind of person*

you'd like *me to be. And you stick on the phrase "belief in her true values"! You've proven you don't even know what that means. You think of me as an image, not a person. "The* real *you—kind, considerate, radiant, lovely, friendly and full of good humor." Did it ever occur to you that I'm OK even if I'm* NOT *kind, considerate, etc.? After such an offensive statement (just because it's all nice words doesn't mean it doesn't offend me—it's a gross* MOCKERY *of me as a person), I'm tempted to send you a long exposé of Sally as a person, to end your hopes totally and forever. But if I did, you'd probably interpret it merely to mean I have "no confidence in myself" when actually I'm willing to accept* ME *no matter how badly I grate on anyone else's values.*

"Till then, we will also try to run away from her awful todays, albeit they still remain with us." What does that mean?? Don't tell me unless you know.

"We are sad—you can make us glad." It's not up to me to make you happy. It's not up to you (anymore) to make me happy. But if you try, be sure it's not just you trying to make me *make* you *happy.*

Mother, next time please write about what YOU *feel instead of what Daddy feels, and what* YOU *are instead of what you hope I would be. Get rid of the idea that everything should be positive in your letters. You've got your mind set that you love me—you assume I'm "good" by your standards. That "real you" description—most of what you write about me could be written just as meaningfully about anyone in the world.*

Sally

Sally is trying to set up an honest, three-way communication among her mother, her father and herself. Starting from her rage over her father's peremptory treatment of her possessions and her friends, she tries to reveal her feelings. She accuses her father of failing to deal with her on the *feeling* level, and indicts her mother for blocking her contact with Daddy by taking over as his interpreter.

Why is Sally exposing herself to counterattack? Why is it important to her to push the communication further than the immediate issue of how Daddy treated her things and how he criticized her friends? Why should she risk any hope for future emotional support by accusing her parents of such serious crimes—"You don't know me; you don't see me; all you want is to be the parents of a certain kind of a daughter!" Sally is not only risking the loss of any future emotional rapport with her parents, but she is also risking the loss of financial support as well, no small loss for a girl in college. Why shouldn't she overlook her father's behavior, treat it as a small incident? Yet she drives the issue down to its fundamentals, raising new and deeper questions about the feelings she, her father and her mother have about each other, and about the power factors in the relationships as well. In short, Sally is attempting to involve both her parents in a three-way communication about:

Issues—the incidents she is upset about.

Feelings—the feelings she thinks lie behind the incidents.

Power—the questions of freedom and obligation in their relationships.

So far, what are the positions of the protagonists in this failed attempt at three-way communication?

Sally, to Daddy:

You don't respect me *or* my property. You treat my things carelessly, sweep them into a heap in the closet, damaging them. And when I call you to account for it, as anyone might, you don't even reply or explain. This all gives me the feeling that if I don't act and become something you want me to be, then you regard me as *nothing*.

Daddy, to Sally:

No reply.

Mother, to Sally:

Daddy and I are sorry for any mistakes we made, though we don't know what they may have been. We love you and want you to be happy. Let's try to forget the past.

Mother, to Sally (indirectly):

We are hurt by your anger and pain—but we can't take it up with you. We can't let our real feelings be known.

Sally, to Mother:

You are afraid to tell me what you really feel about me. You hide behind joint position statements expressed with and for Daddy. And these are full of platitudes and pious hopes. They don't contact *me* at all.

Sally is begging for *real* contact. First she pleads, then she attacks. Her goal is to get to the bottom of what is going on between her parents and herself. Driven by anger and feeling isolated from her parents, she is pressing the issue to the very core. She must find out how they really feel about her and thus cannot accept how they *say* they feel about her. Those platitudes don't begin to explain why her father has acted as he did toward her and why he then withdrew into silence, any more than her mother's sweet generalities explain her position of support for her father. Doesn't her mother understand how Sally felt when her father treated her as he did? Or does she think Sally should overlook it because one shouldn't challenge the basic dogmas of the family:
—Whatever we do to each other, we love each other all the time.
—We never hurt each other except unintentionally.
—Parents can't be happy unless kids are happy, so kids should make parents happy by being happy and productive.
These are the ideas Sally labels bullshit—not because they describe an ideal, but because they are not what is really going on in any family most of the time. Sally is trying hard to make a new kind of contact with her par-

ents. She deserves real credit for trying to put her anger and hurt into words, and to get through to her parents in a way that challenges them to answer her. She is not a child anymore, and she is trying to make an adult-to-adult relationship with her mother and father. It's clear that her relationships with her parents have been full of distance and resentment and disappointed hopes in the past, and she's right to assume that old painful relationships can be changed only if the accumulated feelings can be expressed *and heard* by both sides. Once these old feelings are out of the way, she can take advantage of her parents' years of life experience and the worthwhile advice they might have for her. So, she is right to keep trying, rejecting the responses that don't make sense to her, and asking for replies that are honest and direct.

I also like the fact that Sally is taking responsibility for her own feelings. She can say, "I feel . . ." That might encourage her parents to reply more directly. But she should try to avoid interpreting her parents' motives and intentions. She'd often be wrong doing that.

Above all, I admire Sally's refusal to be *anyone's* Barbie doll. She is in the process of finding herself, and if she is not as sweet and kind and considerate as her mother would like her to be, she is right to admit it and seek the causes of her behavior rather than to accept the sugar-coated pathway back to her parents' acceptance, by acting a part that is not herself. I would not advise her to play the defiant rebel, but to do as she is doing—telling how she feels and why, and trying to get communication *open*.

I wonder if Sally's mother knows how she feels about Sally. She quotes how Daddy presumably feels, she expresses hopes and wishes for Sally, but she doesn't tell her how she feels about her as a person nor does she take up her complaints. Sally's letter was a cry for understanding and contact. It asked, "How do you feel about *me*?" even, "Do you love me?" But Mother didn't reply clearly at all. Is she afraid to disagree with her husband's dismissal of Sally's values and his offhand treatment of her property? If she can't disagree with her husband, she may well be a victim of the vagueness of identity that Sally as a person and a woman is trying to avoid. If, deep down, she is as sanctimonious and unable to see Sally's anguish as her letter suggests, then she herself should try investigating her real feelings and thus becoming more of a real person, and much more honestly available to her family.

Sally can't wait forever for Mother to reach across the gap to her and offer her feelings. If she doesn't do it soon, she may lose her for a long time or forever. And what is Daddy waiting for? If he has reasons for how he deals with Sally's values and her property, he should tell her what they are. If not, he should apologize to her and consider how he can make better contact with her in the future.

I'm concerned that he might be the kind of father who just doesn't get emotionally involved in his family. He does what he does, says what he says, and everybody must live with him or get out. But young people like Sally often do get out. Then their parents lose them. Or if they stay, they hide their resentment and present masks of sweet compromise. Not only does this sweetness not ring true, but it hurts them to be so false. In the end, families don't work when any key member won't communicate at the feeling level. That's what spreads the problems around; emotional symptoms develop, and the psychiatrists end up with more work to do.

Sally's father should think over the fact that his family is in bad shape, and he could help by letting his wife know he can deal with Sally directly, and then confront Sally with how he feels about her. All of it, the love *and* the disagreement. He might consider a few sessions of family therapy, letting an expert help them all learn how to be more honest with each other. Then he could continue on his own. He might even become friends with his daughter.

In the changing relationships within families as children become adults, there are almost daily incidents that arouse strong feelings and cause shifts in the power balance of any family. When teen-agers tell parents they are leaving school or college, traveling far away to "find out what's happening," when young men and women in their early twenties declare they are never going to get a job or get into a career like Dad's, or Mother's, or just can't seem to take advantage of the financial and educational opportunities parents work hard to provide, deep and serious doubts, fears and angers are aroused in parents.

Likewise, when parents announce their first or second separation or divorce, when Dad loses his job or gives it up, when one or both parents attack some course of action a child proposes, deep and serious doubts, fears and angers are aroused in adolescents and young adult children.

All this needs to be dealt with honestly and bravely; families need to communicate over vital issues, over what is really going on in the family. Often as a psychiatrist I have found adolescents and young adults fighting as Sally is to get it *all* out in the open, to get communication going in the family. Some of these attempts fail but many succeed. There *are* ways to become a family again, even when the children are grown and gone or going out on their own. Parents don't have to lose their children when they grow up, nor the children lose the parents when they leave them.

Postscript: Almost two years later, Sally was still involved in her solo campaign to get an honest relationship with her parents, and meeting one defeat after another. Perhaps, she thought, if she started calling her parents by their first names, they might see she wanted them to be just *people* with her. They didn't respond. Her mother said angrily, "You must respect the *roles*, not the people. We're *not* just people to you, we're your mother and father!" This angered Sally so much that she cut off all communication for several months. When her mother visited her unannounced, Sally was still so enraged that she pretended she was not at home and would not let her mother come in. More months passed.

Later, Sally was accepted at a school of nursing. Remembering that her mother had often said, "There's always

money for any *good* thing you want to do," Sally asked for
financial help with nursing school. Her mother agreed but
then called back and withdrew the offer, saying, "We've
decided not to give you the money because you don't want
a relationship with us!" Sally was surprised at how deeply
upset she felt over this. She realized that her desire for
real closeness with her parents was bigger and more important than she had known. She interpreted her mother's
message as: "We will withhold our help from you so long
as you don't relate to us *on our terms*—that means com-
plying with our wishes and not challenging us." Sally decided it was more important to her to achieve honesty in
the relationship with her parents than to get the money for
school, even if it meant she couldn't get there at all. So she
told her mother she wouldn't accept any money anyway.
And there matters rest.

Sally wrote me the other day:

Dear Shep,

> *You asked me to write down my thoughts about fam-
> ilies. I think that the worst thing about my own family is
> that it isn't exceptionally disturbed. Although I rarely say
> so to people, I think that the most damaging parts of my
> own family experience were the most common ones, the
> ways that my parents fit the accepted standards for what is
> good in a family. Ironically, it seems to me that the more
> obvious problems my parents had were what made it
> possible for me to have any identity outside of family
> roles, in that these problems made it harder for them to
> hide the fact that they were people rather than Mother
> and Daddy. While this is what I think is really going on, I
> find that it is not a position most people understand. I
> have a more effective argument against my parents in the
> fact that my mother had screaming fits on a regular basis.
> In situations where I have to explain my relationship with
> my parents to other people, such as roommates, I usually
> say that my mother is seriously disturbed. It bothers me*

that I have to offer this half-truth to people. I wish that it would be enough just to say that I don't want my parents being "roles" to me.

I think that women, especially women over forty, are denied any major outlet for their energy other than their relationships with their children and husbands. This makes it very hard for my mother. She is in a position where she is dependent on me to be the person she wants to be— small wonder that she will go to almost any length (like calling my employer) to avoid losing me. She wants to solve her problems by being a mother to me. When she makes phone calls checking up on me, she comes on as being worried that I'm not OK. I don't think she's really worried that I am OK; she is calling not to take care of my needs, but to take care of her own. She really wants me to take care of her, by sharing my life with her. I don't want to share my life with her. I don't think she will ever be in a position where she'll stop wanting to reaffirm her self-image through her relationship with me. Right now, she really wants to establish herself as superior to me, a person I look up to. This is offensive to me, and I don't feel as if I have any defense from it, short of just denying her access to my life. I think it's really bad for me to expose myself to hearing her say things she has to get out. She's very effective at transferring her anxiety onto me.

I am especially upset that she found out where I work. It bothers me that after I have told her to leave me alone, she can find people who will cooperate with her in checking up on me. If I do get a new job, I probably wouldn't be taken seriously if I told people at this job not to give her any information about the new job.

There is an attitude that's common among middle-class parents that their children don't have a right to resist them. I think my mother relies heavily on this attitude to justify her violations of me. I guess her line of reasoning goes that if I feel I need to resist her, then that shows that I'm unhappy; and if I'm unhappy, then I need whatever it is she's doing. And she can talk with people where I work who agree. Is it any wonder that I feel I have no defense from her?

Sally's struggle with her parents for honest recognition makes me sad because it's probably doomed to fail. Years from now, Sally will still feel she needs to defend herself against her mother, whom she feels wants a particular kind of contact with her just to shore up her own unsatisfying life. And her mother will still be wondering how Sally got so angry and senselessly rebellious when she had parents who were always willing to help her if only she'd be a little bit nice and respectful to them.

In the next three chapters, I will share the stories of some young adults I have known in my practice. Like Sally, these young people felt that the transition from being their parents' children to being *adults* in their parents' eyes was vital to their own growth. They resorted to challenges, confrontations and, in some instances, extreme and self-destructive behavior to provoke encounters that might cause catharsis of old feelings and result in a new kind of friendship with their parents. Out of these struggles I believe some patterns emerge, which can make us more aware of the underlying issues.

CHAPTER 2

"Try to live up to your potential"

Billy, at twenty-three, had dropped out of college in his junior year. After his freshman year, he had taken a year off, developed his piano playing and joined a band. He began composing his own music and considered becoming a musician. This made him feel guilty, since his older brother was already in dental school and Billy's parents were tremendously proud of Jack's progress toward a profession. Under the circumstances, Billy presented his year off to his parents as merely an interlude, and didn't dare tell them that he was becoming serious about music as a career. During his year with the band, Billy started acid-tripping and found it mind-expanding and stimulating to his musical creativity. But under the pressure of the impending return to college, which he dreaded, he tripped over a hundred times. By the time he reentered school, he couldn't focus his mind on studies. They seemed pointless and irrelevant, yet he didn't dare confront his parents' disappointment and his own guilt until he finally quit after his junior year and got into therapy.

Billy's parents tried to get his permission to talk with his therapist, to find out what was happening. Billy resisted this; he feared they'd get the psychiatrist to exert achievement pressure on him. During this time, Billy got this letter from "Mom and Dad," written by Mom.

Brae Mar Hotel
Bermuda
Saturday eve.

Dearest Billy,

This is really a very unusual place—away from people, large buildings, even a town with shops is far away. It's a new resort with 2 golf courses—one called The Angel and one The Devil. You can guess which is the hard one to play. There are homes and cottages built all around the courses. We found it because one of our friends bought a home here last year. They are older than we are—he is 73 (retired druggist). Dad is very tense and doesn't like the same resorts over again—so we stayed in a bigger hotel for a week, then started finding new horizons. But it's the height of the season and you can't go anywhere without reservations. We can hardly believe the trouble we're having. There sure are lots of rich people around here on vacation; I even had to make a dozen phone calls to get a hotel reservation for tomorrow just in case we couldn't get in here. You just wouldn't believe it.

But we're having a fine vacation in spite of all that and the cool weather. Dad is more relaxed now than when we came—he was really wound up at first. One must look at the brighter side of things and though we have to hassle a lot we don't let it get us down.

On the phone the other nite you didn't sound really happy. I hope nothing is seriously wrong. I do hope you are not over-counselling yourself with your psychiatrist and your group. There is such a thing as overdoing and looking inside yourself too much. Dad and I both love you dearly and want to see you being a happy person.

We as parents have always considered you, your brother and sister before considering ourselves. We would do anything in the world to help you find yourself in life and find some direction that would make you a contented person. I feel as an adult that when one finds a direction and a goal in life, one is a much more contented individual.

Even if the goal is but a stepping-stone in some direction, life is better. We know your great potential. We have witnessed it through the years you have lived at home. You are far above most of the kids around you in intelligence, perception, leadership, etc. You must not be your own worst enemy. Of course, if you decide on any walk in life, you must be honest to yourself and hard working and whatever you do will give you lots of satisfaction; to achieve, one cannot be lazy. We worked so hard all our lives to achieve in life what we in our generation thought was the most important thing and that was financial security. I would never want to be poor again, Billy. We suffered too much when we were young, and had nothing. There are certain comforts in life that most people strive for and I don't think everyone is wrong. Life is beautiful and can even be more so when you have some money in your pocket. Please read this letter carefully and give it some thought. We'll call you. Keep well.

> *Love and kisses*
> *Mom & Dad*

Perhaps under the pressure of Mom's worries about Billy's unhappy sound over the phone, Dad wrote Billy a short note a few days later.

Bill—

I know you are struggling to find your niche in our civilized (?) world.

You know Mom and I will never let you down. Try to live up to your great potential. You are basically head and heels above your fellow men—don't sell yourself short.

And remember—there is no love greater than that of a parent for a child.

> *I love you*
> *Dad*

Billy told his therapist:

I never felt I could talk to Mom and Dad about any-thing they didn't want to hear. I'd get smothered with as-surances of love and support, and told I was such a superior person—it made me feel that if I were anything but tops in achievement and ambition, I was letting the team down. Their attempts to talk to me were like the football coach between the halves saying, "Now I know you've got what it takes—get out there and WIN!"

I go home and I hear this, "Don't let us down, we know you're great. So do things our way because we know you can!" This all makes me feel like shit! What have I got to tell them? Things I feel good about like writing my own rock music or getting my head straighter after all those acid trips are things they think are bad. Like what they say about therapy, which means a lot to me—or taking time off from getting a great job to find peace with myself. They even tell me how to do that—by having a goal, stop-ping being lazy, and achieving more, like my brother Jack. They're ashamed that I need therapy and a little fucking part of me is too!

What is really being communicated here?

On the surface, Mom and Dad are giving good advice. Fundamentally they are saying: "Achievement within the structure of society is the right path. We chose it and we are happy with it. We're not poor anymore; we can afford nice vacations. Try it; you'll like it!"

But are they aware that they are telling Billy more?

"Don't look at yourself so much." Since this *is* what Bill is currently doing, he is violating their advice by seek-ing therapy, yet they pay for it. This makes him feel guilty for getting help. "You have no valid reason to be un-happy." Since Bill *is* unhappy, he must believe that some-thing is wrong with him to be unhappy after receiving all that love and support. This love and support feels like achievement pressure to him. If he tells them they're pres-suring him, they deny it; they tell him they'll go along with whatever makes him happy. If he believes that this is love, not pressure, he must be sick, since whenever Mom and Dad talk achievement, he feels pressured and guilty, not loved.

I believe that all three protagonists in this situation are being less than honest—Bill as much as his parents. He needs help to be able to say to Mom and Dad:

"I'm having serious doubts about the whole achievement trip—college to a profession or a high-paying job. I'm going to take time off to decide *if* I accept your advice and your example, or if I don't. If I choose my own path, you have every right not to help me with it if you don't agree with it. I feel too guilty when you disapprove of what I do, yet help me pay for it. Then I'm taking advantage of you, and you're permitting it."

Bill is using his therapy to become more honest with himself about what he really is and what he wants. In order for him to keep up any real relationship with Mom and Dad, he'll need to tell them what he feels even if it's not what they want to hear, and for him to respect them they will need to be equally direct.

I remember at fifteen when I began having second thoughts about entering the tunnel leading from college to medical school to internship to psychiatric residency, I told my mother I might want to go to art school instead. She was already committed to my becoming a psychiatrist, in fact the one who might be able to cure her depression (a terribly serious, lifelong despair) where all others had failed. But she was in the same classic bind as Bill's Mom and Dad and millions of others—she had proclaimed that "I only want you to be happy, in whatever you choose to do." So she ignored my doubts and became more depressed when I repeated them. The next step was taken when I would not stop raising the art school issue. I was taken to a psychological testing agency and given a three-day battery of psychological aptitude and preference tests. To my mother's surprise, the results pointed strongly toward architecture. After this, I was taken to see her psychoanalyst, who shut the door, then informed me in shocked tones that I'd be crazy to become an artist, which was to him the same as a bum—"artists can't make a living, they're nobody in society." Did I want to kill my mother, who couldn't cope with the problems she already had?

My point is not that I'm sorry I became a psychiatrist and not an artist. I have found ways to combine my aesthetic side and my creativity with psychiatry. But my point is that in my family, my mother was less honest than Bill's—she couldn't have it out with me by telling me her own views about my career. *Guilt* was the weapon she used. When I hear, "You have absolutely no reason to be unhappy," the same guilty twinges come back to me to this day.

Bill's Mom and Dad have every right to say out loud exactly what they feel about Bill's career choice. In the days of more universal economic necessity, fathers and mothers *expected* children to take over the farm or the family business or the craft that had been passed down in the family. They made no bones about it. With middle-class liberalism, parents feel guilty these days—they feel it's wrong to say, "We'd love to see you become a doctor or an insurance agent." But if that's what they really feel, it will come out somehow. Bill is picking up the guilt vibrations over his nonachievement, just as I did over art school. I think Bill's parents should be worried over his avoidance of the issue, his reluctance to confront them and the issue that keeps him a guilty child, not a self-directing adult. In this family, somebody needs to start speaking the truth, as Sally is doing with her parents.

Somebody needs to start speaking the truth. This is the feeling expressed to me by a number of young people who can't imagine the perpetuation of these hypocritical relationships with their parents into a lifetime of not being honest with each other. Many of my friends in their forties and fifties now have handled their relationships with their parents in just this way—avoiding telling parents anything that would upset them. This is a technique learned from emotionally dishonest parents and passed on as a major life-skill. When I was planning my marriage, my mother took me aside and whispered to me, "Lois is a *wonderful* girl, but she's not Jewish! That's fine with *me*, of course— but it will kill your father!" And my father confessed to me, also secretly, "I love Lois, but your mother could never stand you marrying a Gentile!" I learned a lot from them in this way, never to reveal what you felt or wanted if it would upset somebody. Also that if you upset somebody, he or she would never admit it, but just get sick.

Billy has that lesson to unlearn, just as I did. If he sticks to avoidance, he'll feel worse than he would if he had no parents at all; the very essence of his values and feelings will not be shared with them—and if not, what's a family for?

If he decides to confront his parents with *their* double messages, he'll first have to see how dishonest he himself is being, and that will be painful. This is why many young adults return to their parents with a new and more honest attempt to relate soon after their own therapy. Having discovered the effects of family dishonesty upon their own style of meeting life, they genuinely want to help their parents find their own way out of the same trap. But parents have been at it longer and often have a vested interest in defending their life decisions and values. Sometimes this is because they genuinely believe in the validity of their lives. Sometimes they must protect themselves from seeing the extent of their own mistakes and inner despair.

CHAPTER 3

Letter of indictment

In order to get communication going with parents, many young adults borrow a technique from adolescence, the stage of development during which one launches oneself from the family into the world. A hallmark of adolescence in our society is the angry outburst against parents: a scathing indictment both of their policies in the family and of their life-style. If parents take this as a childish temper outburst and respond with control measures, they can choke off the beginning of a confrontation that might lead to mutual understanding. Indictments of parents by young people often lead to real communication—if parents listen seriously and try to find the truth underlying the blast.

At twenty-three, Melissa wrote hers down in letter form:

Dear Mom and Dad,

When I started therapy and throughout the course of it, I have continually sworn that I would never indict you for your behavior towards me, that I knew inside that you both struggled to do the best you knew how.

Well, now I am going to indict you. I am crying as I haven't cried in a long time. I can barely see the words as I write them. I ache so much inside. John lies in the other room watching TV and I am in here, miserably unable to do that which I want most in life—express my love for him. All because of you two. . . .

You denied the value of my individual personhood from the beginning. I was supposed to be Charles Hadley III. You always told me that. I always felt inferior for being a girl. . . . From the beginning you two made me think of myself as a undesirable creature until now I feel myself so inferior that when I can't accomplish this task of being able to feel my love for John, I want to kill myself—not as a means of retaliation or in a desperate attempt for someone to pay attention to me—hoping I am a desirable person—but only of futility; a knowledge that I am a pile of shit, and knowing that—knowing—hear me—knowing, not just thinking of it as a possibility but really knowing, and thus not having any desire to live.

Long ago, Mother, you taught me to hate my body and think of sex as evil. So that now and for the past 2½ months I have been denied any awareness of my sexuality. I have been undergoing one of the most intensive forms of therapy, hypnosis, trying to overcome all that, but so far it has only begun to succeed, and I am losing hope. More and more I feel down to the pit of my being that I am worthless.

Daddy, you too are to be indicted. For a long time I have only hated Mommy, and wished her dead, feeling we all would be happier if she were gone so we wouldn't have to constantly hear her criticize us, but you too failed me. When you financially disowned me and disowned me in your heart, when I went to Washington for the peace march, you went crashing off your pedestal. How could anyone who loved me do that to me when I was only standing up for my convictions? Something you had always taught me to do. But the minute my convictions differed from yours, I was not supposed to do that. I was supposed to deny my own personhood in favor of being your robot.

I hope every word of this is searing into your heart. Since that day, you have retreated farther and farther from me emotionally, so that I feel when you touch me you are only a cardboard person.

As long as I do things which you two can boast about to your friends, I am vaguely on the verge of being an acceptable offspring.

As you don't recall, but I do very strongly, I got deathly ill when Granny died. That was because I felt Granny was the only person I have known who unconditionally loved me. Her love for me was not based on whether or not I behaved properly. Right or wrong she still loved me and it was after her death, Mom, when you and Aunt Alice were arguing over who was to get the TV set and I heard that argument through the banisters that I decided it was not safe ever to love someone again—you would only use them or they would hurt you in the long run. . . .

I do love the two of you. I have never been able to successfully divorce you from my heart and soul and hate you for all the shit—your own hang-ups that you never dealt with and instead laid on me.

Even now as John hugs me and consoles me I am angry at you two for not being a loving Mommy and Daddy to me. I am still a little girl inside. I cannot love him as a woman. Mother, I don't think you love Daddy as a woman. You often talk to him in baby talk and need to be sheltered all the time like a helpless infant. I don't think either of you yet see me as a woman. Besides not accepting my personhood you can't accept my womanhood. Mother, you have constantly made me feel guilty about my sexuality, so important a part of being a woman. For so long I used sex as another form of rebelling against you, but now when I want to stop rebelling and give myself to another person, I have lost my sense of sexuality. It's only safe for me to feel sexy with men who are not my equal, who can never return my love for them, with whom I can hold a large portion of myself distant. I want to experience an orgasm with John so badly, yet you do not want me to. He wants to spend the rest of his life with me—a type of marriage commitment, isn't that good enough?—won't

*you release me so I can feel free to experience my sexuality
and orgasm with him? I wonder if I ever will be able to
unless I know ahead of time that you both love me as a
person. And as a woman. And I fear that the only way I
will get that is to come to you after I am sure of my
feelings for him, instead of before. So I feel hopelessly
locked in, how can I ever achieve that act of proudly coming to you and saying I love him and want to spend the
rest of my life with him—if what will let me make those
commitments is only to come after I have made them—
your acceptance of me as a lovable and worthy person*
and woman?

*I guess I need to come to you both and tell you I need
that before I can fully open myself up to John. And hope
that you will give it to me. To say for once that the differences in our life styles can be overlooked and that you
can say you love me.*

*When I ask you, Mom and Dad, please make me feel
it, make me feel that you cherish my life and think I am a
fine person and a beautiful woman. Overlook all the ways
I have disappointed you and just give that to me. Most of
the ways I have hurt you have been a fight to receive just
this. Through the course of writing this my tears have
stopped. I pray you can give me what I need.*

*I have always been afraid of both of you. Afraid of your
reaction when I told you things. That is why I was so
tactless—my fear of how you would react always would
overcome me and make it possible for me to wait until
more appropriate times to spill the tears. This invariably
would mean I would choose the most inappropriate time
and your reaction would justify my fears. It is only in the
past year that I have been able to learn how to control
that. My fear of you both has carried over into many
other situations with many other people. I would get need-
lessly intimidated by professors, teachers, employers, etc.
And with my peers until lately, this past year, I have always
felt totally inadequate. This past year I have developed a
large number of deep friendships with people my age,
which have told me that in their eyes I am a worthwhile*

person, someone they care about. Somewhere very early you both helped me to feel inadequate. . . .

When I was homesick at camp and school and college, you never came to me but told me it was childish. You should have supported me. Those were strong genuine feelings, some of the strongest I have ever felt. And you always said that it was my choice to go to boarding school. True, but can a twelve-year-old really know the most appropriate way to try to make herself happy? No! Did it ever occur to you to take me out of accelerated classes and put me back in the regular program? No! You should have. You would have saved a lot of money and perhaps had a happier child. Peer group acceptance is what I wanted most. Even in dancing school I was always a wallflower, one of the least accepted girls.

I was always afraid of being caught, afraid something was wrong in me and very guilty when I explored my body and played with my genitals as a girl. I remember a couple of times when you caught me in bed nude. That was sinful in your mind. When I discovered masturbation, I thought it was evil and something was wrong with me. I was petrified that you might find out about it, and was scared stiff of your reaction to it.

I'll never forget the night I told you I wanted to see a psychiatrist and how you, Dad, slapped me several times across the face for yelling at Mom. That was sick, downright sick on your part. Here I was pleading for help—all you were offering was your "help." What I was trying to escape from. Your help was not genuine—not to help me as an individual but an attempt to mold me into the person you wanted me to be . . . to be your slave, to fulfill everything the way you people wanted for yourselves, but couldn't accomplish. I am my own person! Live your own dreams! Let me have my own!

I hated the way, Mom, you used to slap Jane around when I was in grade school. Then you would run to your room crying. Daddy, you always went to Jane. And I would be left to comfort Mom, to play parent to my parent. That is about one of the worst things you can ask a

*young child to do for you. That pattern continues to this
very day. Mom, you share your problems with me and
expect me to play parent to you, particularly problems
between you and Dad. You two should be adults and discuss them with each other instead of asking your child to
play messenger and mediator.*

*Even when you ceased to be able to control my behavior,
you have been what I call "mind-fucking" me. Your endless judgments are heard by me. Though possibly ignored
by me in my actions, it eats away at my head. So when
you tell me I should do such and such or am such and
such a way, although I consciously reject it, inside my
head, deep inside, your statements haunt me. Why can't
you leave my head alone and let me have peace of mind?*

*Bill, there's a sore spot. Yes, he was the wrong kind of
man for me. But it would have been easier for me to admit
that to myself, and I would have done so sooner and saved
myself a lot of grief if you hadn't told me time and again
how shitty he was. You were assaulting my integrity, my
judgment, you were saying I was untrustworthy to make
valid decisions, and because of those things I rebelled and
strove to show you you were wrong, that I was a person
with integrity, and sound judgment. By staying with Bill,
who was in fact making me very unhappy. But to admit
that and to leave him would have been to admit all those
things about myself which I couldn't do. Sometimes it's
better to keep your opinions to yourself and to tell the
person that you trust their judgment. Then I would have
been able to change my mind from wanting to be with him,
to being able to leave him! I almost did many times, but
didn't because it would have been giving in to you.*

A week later, Melissa continued:

Dear Mom and Dad,

*On the eve of my birthday, my 25th birthday, I feel the
urge to continue my indictment of you. Today, rather this
evening, and late this afternoon have been, has seen one*

of the happiest times of my life. John at supper, beaming and full of love and surprise gave me a ring and whispered in my ear—"Consider yourself engaged." Though I loved the ring, what he said scared me. And you two are the ones from whom this fear generated. You wonder why all these years I have needed to be so fucking self-sufficient, never to lean on anyone. It's because I learned long ago that if you lean on someone, if you need them or commit yourself to them, they will hurt you when you least expect it and are least prepared for it. They will turn on you. That is what the two of you did to me. You made me feel that I could never fully trust anyone and promise myself to them. I am struggling with this fear. I do not want to feel this shadow my entire life. I want to feel free enough of the evil ways you haunt my head to give myself to John for life.

Today also as I was looking at apartments, I looked at one on Wendell Street. I knew inside that you two would love it and that almost made me take it. Deep inside I want to do things which will make you accept me fully. But the apartment had disadvantages for me like a lease and a nasty landlord, who might cause hassles later when I might want to sublet on the lease.

I want you to STOP *meddling with my head. Leave my head alone!*

I want the feelings I am feeling for John to grow. They are so fragile now. And they are having difficulty growing and that is because you are still mind-fucking me.

Tomorrow, rather today on my birthday, he is giving me a party I think. He has made more of my birthday and made me feel more worthwhile as a person whose birthday should be fully celebrated than I have felt in a long time. You helped to diminish my feelings of self worth. He is helping them to grow again. . . .

Right now, John and I are suffering through a time in which it is very important to me that I set the limits on our physical contact. They are so restrained on my part, Mother, that it would gladden your puritan heart. Do you want to know why this has all happened? It's because very early in my life you two denied me the control of my own body. As early as my feeding and toilet training you took it away from me. And for so long I guess deep deep inside of me that others controlled my body and my feelings, not me. So that now I have to reenact with my lover who must temporarily play father and mother for me, all the stages of body control. I must now have absolute control of my body, and only slowly am I beginning to share that control willingly with another person, one whom I can trust. I should have done all this with you. But you both wrenched the control out of my hands before I really ever consciously had it. I must have that control before I can give it up, surrender it. You see before this I never had the control so I guess John, like every other man I have known, only reinforced my feelings that I did not have control over my own body. I was not sharing my body with him out of my own free will. He was making me do it. Like every other person I've known. And it all started with you both!

You both got so upset by expressions of anger that long ago you made me feel dirty and guilty about anger. And until recently it has been bottled up in me. In the past few weeks I have been having temper tantrums, something I have always yearned to do, but which I could never freely express or act out in your house.

I remember a scene of being in my room and being very angry for some reason, lying prone across my bed, pulling at the tufts on the spread and wanting to hurl bottles or glasses at the wall. Pulling the tufts on the bedspread wasn't a suitable substitute because I knew you would get mad at me if I destroyed your prized bedspreads. You locked up my only anger vents. Well now I've gotten a lot of that anger out of me which has been pent up since my early childhood. I don't remember having temper tantrums. That's how early you both must of gotten to me. In a daydream the other day, I broke every piece of china and crystal in the house and ripped up all of your clothes and jewelry, Mom. That's a lot of anger.

All those years with The Prophet *and letters to you*

pleading you to let me free from your clutches at the end of high school and your only response—you will do what we say until you are 21. FUCK YOU BOTH. *As* The Prophet *says, I do not belong to you. I am a separate person, you are only the bow from which I spring forth. You can only minimally control the arrow's flight and arrival somewhere. But you tried so hard to do both things fully. You tried to style me.*

Well, I am trying to set myself free inside as well as outside. And I will do it! The reward waiting for me, John, if I can do it, far surpasses the discomfort I have to go through to do it. And I intend to do it. I don't want either of you haunting my head.

The year 25 marks my beginning and hopefully the successful accomplishment of it all. I will *do it! Not as a rebellion against you. But as my birthright as a human being.*

Melissa never sent these indictments. She used them to help her get the feelings out so she could see what the feelings were. Later, she said:

My father abdicated his own happiness, gave up the fight. He went into work he didn't love because it meant more income. His whole life has been settling for what he could get, not trying for what he wanted. That makes me feel sorry for him. I used to want to take him from Mommy and help him better than she can.

I want him to deal with his feelings about what I want and what I do, not just to give me things I ask for. With Mommy I can blunder, she'll end up dealing with the issue better than he will. With Daddy, unless I pick the exact right moment to approach, he won't get involved. The conversation will be empty and I'll leave empty. My only real contacts with him were when I got him angry, like by doing something really bad. But that was rare. His expressions of love for me are so brief I can hardly feel them. I want more of his feelings to relate to.

When he disowned me for going to the Peace March, I

had to sweat long and hard to make my decision. And then
when he gave his controlled speech of disownment, I shut
up and quietly accepted it. I felt if he won't accept me as I
am with my own beliefs, why should I show him my
feelings?

I see I have such power to hurt Daddy. Why is that so?
What do I mean to him? I don't want to hurt him so
much.

We all start off in bondage to our parents. In earliest
childhood, they are the world to us. All trust in human
beings and all hope of love and good feeling from relationships come from them. And by their values, we as
children come to feel we are good or bad human beings.
Melissa is starting on the long road toward finding out she
is a separate person from her mother and father. Stage one
is realizing she is not worthless because she does not
agree with their values and judgments. She wants to enjoy
her body and to *feel* her feelings. She wants her life to be
one of reaching for what she wants, not settling for what
looks available. Inside, she feels the need to indict her
parents for how they limited her by implanting judgments
that clash with who she wants to be.

Will it help if she mails these indictments? Will it merely
hurt her parents more? That depends on their ability not
only to deal with her accusations and her rage, but also
their willingness to look at the limitations of their own
lives. When your adolescent says, "You have hurt me!"
you must face the possibility that you may have done that.
And that's a big step. At this stage it's the child forcing the
parent to grow.

As it worked out, Melissa never mailed the letters. But
she went on to set up face-to-face conversations with both
parents in which she told them who she is and what she
wants from them. Her mother heard her out, replied honestly, and their relationship became more honest. With
her father, things are still in process and in question. Another striking fact—every time Melissa sees how she re-
mains internally enslaved by her parents' judgments of her,

every time she understands her childish needs to please them, she takes steps to break that bondage. This indictment of her parents and her denunciation of their ways of controlling her are not merely adolescent charades; she *must* find ways to show herself *in real life* that she can and *will* change from good little girl to real live woman. Like Sally, she needs to stop being anybody's Barbie doll, and she has to show her parents she's making the change. The deep need young people feel to make these changes and to let their parents know they have changed is a fact of development.

Indictments and denunciations are often the first step in an attempt at communication—Sally, Melissa and Henry and Dan in later chapters all felt the anger first—but they all want to work past the anger to reach the stage where they feel good being what they are, not what their parents want them to be. If the parents are smart, they'll look seriously at the charges and reply with equal honesty. The goal is exactly what parents *say* they want: for the young adult child to become independent and self-reliant. But if parents unconsciously need their childen to approve of them and make them feel secure by living the way the parents live, then they can't reply honestly. They often give double messages: "All we want is for you to be happy!" while actually condemning the acts and decisions that are making the child happy. Later chapters will show in more detail how parents can respond to indictments.

CHAPTER 4

Graduation speech

Emily's parents are about fifty years older than she is. Now that she is starting medical school, they are in their mid-seventies. She has never felt that she could talk freely to them, particularly her mother, on any subject of intimacy—sex, love, anger—"the vital stuff."

Recently, planning to see her parents during school vacation, Emily received two letters from her father. Some of the essential contents were:

Dear Emily,

Our last vacation together was not exactly a triumph! But, I hope we can try it again in the future under happier skies. In parting, you will remember I made several suggestions that I had repeated before. That you stand on your own two feet and stop seeing psychiatrists. In the final analysis you must and will solve your own problems!

We must find contentment in ourselves. It is useless to seek it elsewhere—don't waste your time on yesterdays. You must think of yourself and you can. Stop blaming your loneliness and resentment on your family! There is nothing you can do about it except to be happy and contented and work hard to achieve your aim, to be at the top of your profession. Use that knowledge and skill and

*achievement in any field you choose—only that can bring
you reasonable satisfaction, achievement & contentment.
Stay on that road and don't stumble, and let nothing and
no one divert you from that road. As Freud said when he
was asked what in his opinion is the best in life, his
answer: "Work and love"— And love doesn't mean* free
*love, it means finding a mate that you respect and is re-
spected by society—having children and living a useful and
worthwhile life. Leave all this unhappiness behind you and
live in today and tomorrow, not yesterday. You have made
mistakes—many—nobody can have a sign on their door
"Nothing wrong here" but to repeat the same mistakes is
folly. You have been free to live your own life since
choosing your college. That's all behind you now you are
certain what you want.*

*You are mature, so build that kind of life and world
and friendships you respect—and can emulate! Don't run
from life—life is wonderful and achievement is challenge!
Don't look back, because you can't do anything about it.
And guard your health. Tomorrow's another day. Begin
it serenely, in high spirits, and set high goals for yourself.
You have already proven for yourself that "The difficult
is easy. The impossible will take a little longer!"*

*Life is meant to be lived and work is the most important
part of life. That's the way to live forever. Destiny is not
a matter of chance, it's something to be achieved. You
can and you will.*

*Just a word more—be considerate and tactful with
Mother. She is not well, and she loves you regardless of her
emotional upsets. You are young and as you go through
life, tact and diplomacy and consideration are essential.*

From the second letter:

*I want to caution you. —You and Mother are both in-
clined to argument and anger. Mother is not in the best
of health physically or emotionally, not at her best, as you
well know—and you too are inclined to lose your temper
and become emotionally upset. You must promise to your-*

self, no matter what the provocations, be calm and reason calmly, whatever the subject may be. It will make the difference for our happiness, for our time together. Serenity of mind and calmness are better than any possessions. When we cannot find contentment in ourselves and among ourselves and those we love, we cannot find it elsewhere. Let's be sure to enjoy our vacation together. No arguments—no anger—only calm and enjoy being together. See you soon.

Love,
Daddy

Emily's reaction to these letters was hate and frustration. After receiving each of them she got stoned for days.

What can I do? They don't know what I'm angry about. I never can get to real issues with them—Daddy means well, but he preaches at me. He could say most of that to anyone. I don't feel he knows me as a person; he wants to mold me into a calm and unthreatening child in order to protect Mother! He has always put her first, and tried to protect her from any stress. She rules the family with her nervousness!

Emily went on to talk about her lifelong problem of trying not to be like a mother who couldn't stand stresses or controversy, needed always to be protected by her father, who kept any "unpleasantness" from reaching her mother's ears. How could Emily find out what a strong woman is like? How could she learn that a woman can deal with anger, grief, disappointment? Perhaps because her own mother is her father's "patient," Emily finds that she too avoids acknowledging her feelings and finds it safer to stay stoned on marijuana than to face any inner unpleasantness.

It is hard to know what advice would be realistic here. Emily's father is using the same technique as Sally's mother—protecting the other parent like a child. I know that when my father or mother's psychoanalyst used that device, I felt I had no way to go—I had to swallow the feelings. When I wanted to go to art school, "It would kill your Mother," and when I wanted to marry my wife, the same words were said. I know that deep inside me, I wanted to scream, "Then let it kill her! Can't I ever do anything she doesn't want? Her nervousness rules this family!"

But Emily's parents are in their seventies, the far side of a gulf of fifty years from their daughter. In our time this is a very long cultural gap to bridge. Brought up between 1900 and 1920, their values are bound to be very different from Emily's, and besides, they seem to lack the energy and stamina to face the task of communicating with her. Peace is what Daddy wants, and peace is what he insists Mother needs. To Emily this reads "shut up" except for inoffensive pleasantries.

My advice to Emily was to spill the feelings about Daddy and Mother in therapy first, to find out what these feelings were and where they came from. She had in fact felt her childhood to be an emotional icebox—with few friends her own age, fifteen years younger than her only sister, she never found out much about how to be anything but nice and quiet. Once Emily finds out what her feelings are toward her parents, she must then decide whether she will try to provoke a real emotional encounter to relieve the tension between them, particularly between herself and her mother. She may decide this can never happen because her mother is too protected by her father and he won't listen, preferring to give undeniably good but sanctimonious advice. How can you have a real dialogue with a graduation speech?

Emily left for medical school at about this point. I don't know how far she got in her decision to encounter the real issues with her parents. The outcome seems doubtful. Yet, in other instances which I will describe later, some young people who tried and failed to make a solid emotional contact with parents nevertheless described a feeling of relief, of a burden removed after the attempt. "At least

I had the guts to try, and did my best—that makes me feel like an adult!"

Many parents, particularly older ones, have absolutely no precedent for allowing their kids to speak to them as equals. Brought up in the days of "respect your elders," they lived in a postcognitive society. This is a term Margaret Mead uses to describe the more traditional system in which the older people define the roles and values of a society for the young. This pattern is changing lately in Western societies, at least as far as young people are concerned—but it makes the exchange of honest feelings even more difficult across the generations.

After forty-five years with his wife, Emily's father has learned the habit of protecting her, out of love for her and perhaps out of the need to keep unaware of his own dissatisfaction with her. If he listens to Emily's anger with her, he might awaken his own. Let sleeping dogs lie, he feels. Many marriages hold together at the cost of the mental health of the children. If parents deny their own bad feelings for each other, the kids often feel crazy and guilty when they themselves feel deep anger with one or both parents. "My parents don't seem to feel this way, so what's wrong with *me*?"

As a rule problems *between* members of a family become problems *within* one or more members of the family when expression and working out of feelings is blocked. For this reason, Emily needs at least to *try* to open the issues up. She should prepare her parents by telling them her goal is to get the family closer and more harmonious. Perhaps this might help them to hear her.

It is well understood by those who study families and human emotional development that problems between adults of a family *become* problems *within* the personality of children raised in that family. Parents are Gods—if a father says a mother is all right and you should respect her, then the child feels his or her rage with her is out of place and must be forced down inside. And Emily is not the only child who deals with inner rage at parents by getting stoned a lot. Marijuana is the tranquilizer of adolescence and young adulthood. One young man put it well: "I felt wrong and guilty all my life for feeling the way my father pretends he doesn't feel about my mother— deprived and enraged! Yet when I even hinted at these feelings, he told me I was ungrateful and selfish. If they can't be honest, how do I know what's real to feel?"

In a very serious way I tell parents— "It's you who teach your children what's okay to feel. If you hide deep and vital feelings, your children will try to hide theirs, but worse, they'll feel guilty and wrong for *having* those feelings. This builds into a sense of being basically bad. Once that's built into a child's personality, it's very hard to get rid of."

Parents who hide their real feelings from themselves and their children often resort to raising them by sermons and graduation speeches, not about what *is,* but about what *ought* to be. This simply does not teach children how to express and deal with the unpleasant inner feelings we all have.

PART TWO

Adult to adult

CHAPTER 5

Pouring out
the old feelings

At thirty Henry is tall and strong. He projects intelli*
and emotionality and strong needs for closeness and
interaction. Henry is developing into a psychotherap*
has built his career around the belief that there *
in getting close to people and that love is possib!*

I was raised without much guidance or idea *at I
might become. Some people are socialized to b* *thing
specific—I wasn't socialized to be anything.*

I think my father was a monster. As far *s I can
remember any interaction with him put* *line the
question of my survival. This process sta* *ien I was
five or so and went on till I was twe* *e—then it
continued internally. I believe my fa* *ated me. I
consider myself a battered child. (His* *died when I
was four—and my father blamed hi* *in many ways
because he chose a poor doctor to* *for my grandfather.) He felt a lot of guilt. I think* *ssured him too. I
was probably not the easiest child i* *world to care for.
Also the relationship between my* *er and father was
deteriorating; often my father w* *ent his rage toward
my mother on me rather than d* *y to her. I absolutely
detest my mother—I hate her* *than anyone I know.
She wouldn't protect me from* *father's rage.*

When I was young I used to ride my bicycle around the streets of Chicago until three in the morning because I dreaded and hated going home so much. I never felt loved. I used to go to my mother with the welts on my back from my father's beatings and her comment would be, "What do you want me to do, get a divorce?"

I feel more pity for them these days. I have put a lot of energy into trying to relate to them honestly during the past year or so. An important time for me with them came somewhat over a month ago. There was to be a Bar Mitzvah to which everyone was going. I had resolved not to go. But my family called saying they had been up all night talking about me, and that my father had come in from California just to see me. (My entire family is now enormously guilty over how they scapegoated me—they would do almost anything for me now.) I hadn't seen some of them for about two years. I decided to go down— primarily because I wanted to see my father and complete unfinished emotional business. Last time we talked, I asked him why the beatings and the other stuff. He said he "didn't remember." I then told him that he had better do some soul searching, that I couldn't accept his evading my anger by "not remembering" how he failed me as a father.

One of the big issues for me at this point was how I was going to resolve my "internalized family." I have very sadistic feelings toward my family and these feelings make me feel guilty. I want to resolve these feelings. I don't want to carry them around anymore. They spoil my life.

My father is going blind. He told me that when the day comes that he is totally blind, that is the day he is going to kill himself. He begged for my forgiveness, for his attacks when I was little; he came and put his arms around me, begging that I forgive him. I felt such a mixture of feel- ings—I remembered when I had felt helpless in front of him—at this moment he was helpless; I felt tremendous ambivalence toward him. I said, "Dad, I don't think I would grieve your death—I won't plead with you not to commit suicide. There have been many nights when I have wished you were dead." I told him how I used to dream about killing all of them—how I would do it, get them all before I got caught. He was dazed by what I said, it was that stark. He couldn't imagine that much hate in me. He knew things were bad, but he didn't know they were this bad—he didn't realize how deep my hate was. He wanted to give me money. "Look, Henry, whatever you feel about me—live for yourself, take my money and go to school."

My father obsesses about me now. When I was twenty-two, I was told that I would have six months to live (I had tuberculosis). I went into the hospital for surgery; had a temperature of 105 degrees for weeks; got pneumonia and pleurisy from the surgery—in short, very nearly died. I wouldn't let my father come to visit me. I used to accuse my mother of bringing his stench in because she slept with him. He suffered enormously then. I told them all that I wanted to die with dignity and peace—something they never let me have when I was living. Up until the last two years I have never known more than maybe five minutes—in total—of happiness. I was solidly and completely depressed. Things were beginning to pick up right before I got TB. I was making money, women were beginning to see me as a man, I had begun to have hope about my life. Nowadays, I even expect to feel good— I am optimistic, with reservations.

The other thing that happened at the Bar Mitzvah was an encounter with my brother. You should understand some things about my brother first. My brother looks for magical father figures—he met a man who was like this for him. He invested a great deal of our family money in this man's company and lost everything. He destroyed himself and half of the family financially. He felt quite suicidal at the time. I told him I wanted my money back. If he was going to die, I wanted it before. My other brother was quite angry with me for pressuring him at this time. Anyway, this brother used to invite me to his house for dinner. But he always laid down rules like dress nicely, be pleasant, etc. Always trying to orchestrate my life. It made me very angry.

At the Bar Mitzvah, he put his hand on my shoulder,

saying, "*You can always come to my house for dinner. . . .*"
*This remark seemed to trigger all the anger I felt from
the past. I threw his arm off my shoulder and told him I
never felt that I was a real member of this family, that
I felt like an animal who was always kicked around and
had no rights or privileges. Well, my brother had been
drinking, and this, combined with the emotional shock
of my anger, gave him heart fibrillations and he had to go
to the hospital. In the morning, when they were going to
visit the brother in the hospital, my other brother decided
I shouldn't go. I blew up saying, "This shit is going to
stop. I* WILL DECIDE. *You have always decided for me, but
no more."*

*In the end I did not go; I hung around the house for
a while, waiting for a call from my father to tell me when
he was coming back to take me to the train. He called
so late that all the trains had gone and I had to hitch out
full of unresolved feelings, guilt, a kind of paralysis. A
couple of weeks ago I got a call that my father would be
visiting my brother who lives in Boston and that I could
call if I wanted to talk to him. I was still full of my anger
(rage flips me out). Now for the first time I took charge
of this anger—I jogged every day; I refused to let the
anger obsess me—I controlled it. I missed my final con-
ference with my father so everything is still unresolved.
Yet, I am realizing that I can and must decide whether
my life is going to sound like a tin whistle or a symphony
orchestra. I must detach these huge feelings from my
parents and live in the here and now. To do that I feel I
must have it out with my father, my mother and my
brothers. When all the old feelings have been poured out,
I can turn to the future.*

Henry has huge anger. And he has enormous guts. He is
not going to let those who picked on him off the hook.
Obviously, there is revenge here. But there is also inner
realization that so much energy is going into thinking
about his parents, wondering why they hurt him, fanta-
sizing revenge, displacing anger and neediness onto other

people that Henry cannot operate in his present adult life
while this burden is still upon him. He must drop the
burden. He has found he cannot drop it by ignoring it.
He has tried following Emily's father's advice—also Sally's
mother's. "Forget yesterday—live for today and tomorrow." But it simply doesn't work. Henry must work
through the feelings, experience them, share them with
his family, before he can live in the emotional here and
now. And after each family encounter, he works in his
therapy to understand where he stands and where he is
heading. After each unburdening, he feels lighter and
his present life goes better. His family also treats him
with much more respect now.

Unlike Henry, Peter is quiet and reserved. He is very
intelligent and a serious scholar in mysticism and Oriental
philosophies. At twenty-five he is just beginning to define
his own life-style. He lives in an old house he is remodel-
ing himself. He takes joy in performing each task: carpentry, plastering, refinishing. He is filling the house with
Oriental things that have historical and religious meaning—prayer rugs, bronze deities.

While Peter was growing up, his father was in the process of becoming a millionaire lawyer. On the board of one,
then two, then many major companies, the father made
his way up from poverty to riches. Peter and his two
sisters stayed at home with their mother, who became
seriously alcoholic during Peter's early childhood and
stayed that way until he was an adult. Peter remembers
his loneliness and his fear, playing in the quiet house or
reading a book, knowing that his mother was in bed behind her closed door, drinking herself into a semicoma.
He learned to know the sound of her body sliding off the
bed onto the floor. For years all this was a family "secret."
Peter's father took refuge in his work, paid for doctors
and tried to keep the family group together from the outside. Not a close or intimate person, he stayed at a dis-

tance from his children and arranged for them to go to good prep schools in their early teens. Even when Peter expressed his distaste for these Ivy League institutions with their dress codes, compulsory chapel attendance and focus upon academic achievement and team sports, Dad held firm that Peter could not come home. What was there for him at home anyway? His mother was in hospitals as much as out, and when she was home, she couldn't care for her kids. Dad was working constantly.

Peter remembers one teen-age Christmas when he and his father and sisters set up a tree, got presents, then carried Mother downstairs—an attempt to feel like a family. Mother could only weep. She was humiliated to be confronted by their needs for closeness, for a family feeling, for a mother she could not be. Christmas was a disaster.

During all his childhood and adolescence, Peter could never bring himself to talk to anyone in the family about what was going on. What is wrong with my mother? Why can't anything be done about it? Why is my father absent? Does he expect me to care for her when I'm at home, or does he even know how frightening it is to be here with her when she's drunk? Above all, does he know what I'm going through? And what is he feeling? Judging by how little they communicated their feelings, the members of Peter's family were strangers.

Peter remained out of touch with his feelings. Bothered by sadness and nameless distress, he took to heavy drug use and dropped out of school. Marijuana, hashish, cocaine and so on; then he tried to be a rock musician and gave that up too.

Then one summer some of the buried anger and frustration welled up in an irresistible tide, and Peter lost control for a few weeks. He became aware of wanting to murder his father. After a short hospitalization, Peter took a step forward in his therapy and started to deal with his feelings more directly.

As Peter's therapist, I came to feel some of his deep childhood needs for a real father. He turned to me at the peak of his psychosis and wanted to immerse himself in a closeness that would protect him from his anger and his loneliness. He had never before allowed himself to feel such needs for another human being.

As part of his recovery, Peter began to feel a powerful need to encounter both his parents and ask them questions about why their lives had been as they were. Not sure in his mind why it was important to reach out to his parents after years of living apart, he still felt it was emotionally necessary. Peter's style is very different from Henry's: no encounters full of rage and denunciation, no eyeball-to-eyeball stuff. Peter asked me to set up sessions in which he could come to my office with his father, then later his mother, and explore gently how open they could be about their lives together. Peter asked and received my assurances that we would not hurt either parent, particularly his mother, who had at last stopped drinking and was making a new life for herself. So I was able to be present as Peter tried to understand and thus become closer to each parent.

With his father, Peter took up the issue of how sad and lonely the years with Mother's alcoholism had been. The indirect question was, "Dad, why didn't you help me more with it?" He found his father had really loved his mother and had felt equally destroyed and helpless to cope with her drinking. He had retreated into work and paying for her therapy. It was clear that he could not then and could not even now discuss any of the possible causes of her condition. At the very moment when he seemed about to break through and acknowledge his own sadness and feelings of loss, his eyes filled with tears and he said abruptly, "Peter, if you just got a haircut, changed the way you dress and got a steady job—in a bank perhaps— you'd feel so much better!" His plea, though not said in so many words, was the same as Emily's father's: "Look to tomorrow, forget the past!" That's where it ended.

With his mother, we were even more cautious. She simply could not come near any feelings that might have led her to drinking. Marriage problems? Loneliness while

Daddy was out getting rich? Problems from her own childhood? Peter will never know. What she could talk about was her present new life—a new place to live, a new job since her divorce.

I thought Peter would be deeply disappointed in our failure to communicate openly with either parent. But, as we talked after these sessions, he clearly felt that, whatever the outcome of these meetings, he, as an adult, had tried to make the bridge, and that there seemed no point anymore in pressing the matter. Having tried hard and having faced his own fears of these encounters, Peter could now look forward to today and tomorrow, which he could *not* do till now. With a new lightness and freedom, he was able to give up drugs, to develop some skills, and to feel more like an independent adult.

To me, the psychiatrist looking on, the midwife of this process, it seemed clear that the *attempt itself* represented a developmental step—a milestone for Peter and for Henry. If either set of parents had been able to share their feelings with these young men, there could have been new and real relationships built from here; but because they could not, there will probably be distance between them forever. But *the confrontation is in itself a goal,* whatever its outcome.

Later, Peter saw his father again under difficult circumstances—as Peter tells it:

There is a family story about my father when he was eighteen or nineteen years old. He was in deep trouble, on the verge of a nervous breakdown. He went to the family doctor who advised my father to get some help. When he told his mother, she slapped him twice across the face and said, "This family can't afford a nervous breakdown." So my father got a job and went to night school and eventually became extremely successful.

The last time I saw my father was a very strange trip. It was at the beginning of March and I got home to find a note on my door saying that my father was in the

*hospital and that a plane ticket had been reserved for me
on the next plane. My father had chronic digestive trouble
and drinks constantly from morning till he goes to bed—he
has a drink before he has breakfast. His friends and new
wife are really concerned. Anyway, they took him to the
hospital because they were so concerned with his physical
health; they thought he needed a "rest." The next morning
at the very moment that the doctor was making his rounds
and coming into my father's room, my father had a stroke.
They got him a respirator immediately and that saved his
life—he would most likely have died had he not been in
the hospital already. I arrived the next day after this happened and he was still in a semicoma and hallucinating.
He was still in the intensive care unit and had to be restrained because he kept trying to pull out the respirator
tubes. And as soon as he regained his consciousness, he
started giving orders: "Bring me my shoes and a Scotch
and soda." I told him he was too sick, and that nobody
was going to bring him a Scotch and soda. He wanted to
go home—he had a perfectly nice home—and not stay
in any damn hospital.*

*I was deeply reached by this whole thing—here my
father nearly died and the most significant conversation we
had was the skirmish over his socks and shoes and
Scotch. He would always minimize something dramatic;
the whole two weeks I was there we didn't say much of
significance. I was deeply worried that this could happen
again at any time and tried to talk with him about it. His
wife did as well—in fact we both spent about six hours
a day doing family therapy, trying to figure out a way to
help him. I felt he was emotionally out on a limb—he
didn't get along that well with his present wife because
they bickered all the time, and I knew he was still feeling
a lot for my mother (whom he hasn't seen for four years).
Even though he didn't say anything, I'm sure my concern
registered. I said, "Dad, this could happen to you at any
time, and it would be an incredible loss for me if you
should die." I think it meant a lot to him that I spent so*

*much time there—even though all he asked me for was to
run errands. I would arrive at the hospital and he would
greet me with, "Peter, I want you to . . ."*

*The doctor said that if he kept up his heavy drinking the
next time he had a stroke, he could be permanently paralyzed. His response was to talk about getting some guns to
protect his property from thieves, or perhaps shoot himself—he didn't talk about giving up drinking.*

*All the time we were doing this "family therapy" and
trying to get him to see a psychiatrist, I had the sinking
knowledge that this was all about fifty years too late. We
brought in someone for him to see and his response was
to tell the story of his grandfather during Prohibition. The
story goes that his grandfather saw the laws coming and
bought a huge stash of Scotch which lasted him the entire
dry time. He lived until he was eighty-seven and died on
the toilet. (Which for some reason my father considered
significant.) My father is extremely resentful of psychiatrists—he feels they get exorbitant fees for doing nothing. The first time my mother went to one—years ago—
she sat for forty-five minutes and didn't say a word. The
doctor told my father it was an impossible case and that
it would take a quarter of a million dollars to do anything.
My father is very heavy into the work ethic—he has been
working incredibly hard for forty-five years, and he can't
bring himself to pay for therapy.*

*I have a very different relationship with my mother. I've
always thought that she was sensitive and warm—I guess
it is because she could never say no to us kids. She was
lenient while my father was abrupt and disciplined. (We
called my mother after his stroke, and although she
wanted to be kept informed right away, she wouldn't
come to see him, and she never did communicate with
him.) I recently spent two weeks with her at her home
in Delaware—she makes it comfortable to be with her,
though sometimes I get bored; it is peaceful and I can
read and talk with her about music or art. We have nice
dialogues.*

I have never had a falling out with my mother—we

*have never talked about her alcoholism, even though I
visited her for seven or eight years in the hospital. The way
her drinking finally came up between us was bizarre. I
was sixteen and in the kitchen making something to eat
for my mother who was ill in her room. My father and
sister were talking in general about alcoholism, and my
father said in passing, "Well, you both know I guess . . ."
I became extremely upset—"No, I don't know what in the
hell you are talking about!" Of course I knew something
was really wrong, and at that point I hooked things up.
But what got to me was that my father didn't realize that
he had never said anything to me about her problem all
these years.*

*My own struggles have been unalterably affected by all
this. I was on drugs (including coke) for nearly five years,
using them every day. I have been emotionally poverty-
stricken, but now I'm beginning to take life from a positive
view and to enjoy things.*

Peter realizes that he is more aware of his feelings now
than either of his parents are of theirs; this caring for both
his parents is genuine—if you didn't know who was speaking, you might take it that he was his parents' parent.

Peter has reached this level of maturity the hard way.
First, he had to acknowledge his own despair and need for
help. Then he had to *experience,* not just *talk about,* his
rage and neediness, his feelings of abandonment and isolation as he struggled through his childhood and adolescence without an inkling as to what was really going on in
the family, much less *why* his parents were behaving as
they were. One of the major milestones in Peter's growth
from drug-habituated adolescent to responsible adult was
his encounters with his parents, which he felt the need to
set up and to do cautiously, carrying out the delicate task
of seeing how much emotional contact could be made with
each of them, and trying to make that contact.

At the time of the sessions with Peter's father and
mother, I was still unaware that the need to reestablish a
deep contact with parents is a normal part of growing

up—thus I was cautious, even predicted to Peter that we would probably not get far with either of them. But Peter stubbornly clung to the plan, even voiced anger at me when I had to postpone one of the family sessions. In the end, Peter showed me what I now believe to be a truth about young adults: Everyone needs to go back and check out his or her parents as adults, and see how he or she gets along with them. Also, each young adult needs to see how his or her parents get along with him or her as he or she now is—an adult who no longer depends upon them.

I discussed Henry and Peter in the same chapter in order to underline the fact that the *process of trying to make honest emotional contact* with one's parents is valid and vital in its own right, even in families where the results are nil in terms of dialogue between the generations. Henry and Peter were both heavily damaged in childhood by family pathology. Both came to realize, each on his own, that, in order to live in the present, an attempt at confrontation had to be attempted. For both of them, the process was a big step toward health despite small results in terms of open dialogue with their parents.

CHAPTER 6

The final weaning

In my practice, I was fortunate enough to encounter a man who put into a long correspondence the entire process of establishing a new relationship with his parents. When I read these remarkable letters, I could see that they documented the enormous importance of renewed contact between an adult child and his parents. Dan literally worked on this for a good part of his life. He couldn't rest until he had found a way to connect with his parents and make them understand how he felt. As with Peter and Henry, it seemed even more important to him than to many other people because there had been such a difficult family situation, full of attack and counterattack, rage and guilt. In such cases, guilt is the spur. The grown child, tormented by the inner feeling of badness fostered by the sick parent-child relationship early in life, *must* find a way out, to explain and justify his or her feelings and behavior. He or she *must* make parents recognize their complicity in the agony their child has gone through, make them take at least part of the responsibility. This factor—the guilt feeling, the sense of inner badness, gives a sense of desperate pressure to the scenario between child and parents. Dan, who was already thirty when the correspondence began, couldn't keep on avoiding the issue. It cost him too much inside. Like Henry, he had to battle it out, stage by stage.

When he was twenty-nine, Dan wrote his mother a letter which he characterizes as a "declaration of isolation":

Dear Mother,

As I mentioned previously in a letter I mailed to you a few weeks ago, Janet and I definitely do not want to attend another tension-filled holiday together. Contacts with members of the family merely serve to remind me of the conflict and suffering I experienced as a child. I always find such occasions to be extremely upsetting.

Janet and I are seeking to build a new life of our own— one in which unpleasant events are replaced with happy, rewarding ones. An important part of this is creating our own holiday traditions. We want to have Thanksgiving and Christmas in our house with just our children and friends. I guess you might say that the final weaning process has taken place and we desire to be totally independent, living a life that satisfies our particular needs and desires. This is especially important to me since I am now at age 29 finally recovering from the psychological damage I experienced as a child, and I emphatically do not want my children to have to suffer through the same experiences I encountered.

It is a bitter thing to have to say, but I do not want to have even an occasional contact with you. I want to achieve inasmuch as it is reasonably possible a complete break with the past. Let's not bother giving each other gifts any more. The whole thing has developed into a needless atonement for unconscious guilt feelings anyways, and it's about time it stopped. Take that same sum of money and spend it on something you enjoy. You work hard to earn it; you might as well spend it on yourself and get some direct pleasure out of it.

I know you will never understand why it is so important to me that I achieve this total independence. There would be nothing gained in even trying to explain the reasons, and certainly that would make everyone quite unhappy. I do hope that you will respect my wishes and not try to interfere.

Dan

This letter opened a long period of isolation from his parents and the end of superficial contact. Dan found this better than hiding his feelings about his childhood, when he was beaten and neglected.

Three years later his mother wrote:

Dear Dan,

Our separation from you becomes harder as time goes on. The happiness of my children has always meant more to me than anything else, and, if I have made mistakes, they were unintentional.

Of course, it's not unusual for me to cry, but if you had seen your father sobbing at Christmas time whenever he heard a carol, you might have felt a little sorry for him. I wake up in the night with the feeling that I might die without ever seeing you again. After all, I'm 71 and Dad and I both have ailments.

Friends cannot take the place of one's own children, and I hope that your children will never desert you when you need their affection most.

So I won't write to you again, but I want you to know that if you ever find it in your heart to forgive whatever I have done that's wrong, we both love and miss you and all your family very much indeed.

Mother

Sometime after this letter, communication reopened between Dan and his parents. Six years later, Dan wrote another letter:

Dear Mother and Dad,

I have been thinking about our recent visit at your apartment and I wanted to say some really nice things. Since you enjoy getting letters, I thought I'd send you a note.

For some wonderful reason, both of you have mellowed in your old age. Instead of becoming even more argumentative and cantankerous, you have somehow learned to get along with each other in a kind and loving way. Perhaps it was the absence of all your sons that allowed you really to adjust to each other as you have. I know that many of the household arguments centered around conflicts over discipline or the competition for attention and affection. There was also the financial drain of supporting a family in rather lavish style—on a not so affluent budget. That, too, must have contributed to the strain. The result was that all too often when the family was together there would be fights (some of them quite violent). There was always an undercurrent of hostility which was very upsetting. What a contrast to visit you now and not hear a single insult, not an angry word . . . to be greeted with smiles and consideration, and equally important—to see both of you treating each other in the same manner. You cannot imagine how good this makes both Janet and me feel! You probably have no idea how much more pleasant it is for us to see you both under these conditions.

Mother, you used to have a particular characteristic which drove me out of my mind (literally as well as figuratively). This was your need to run everything and everyone you came into contact with. If you didn't like the way that I did something (or the way that I looked, dressed, made love to my wife, brought up the children, etc. etc. . . .), you would conduct the most powerful, insidious campaign to change my way that any human could possibly do. This technique included direct confrontation, subtle indirect comments, endless non-verbal manipulations, and, if necessary, even secret pacts with others (who would then assist you in getting me to do what you wanted!). This whole process so unhinged me that I sometimes did not even know when the thing that I was doing was a result of my own desires. Often, I would catch myself carrying out your wishes, satisfying your needs—just as if you had cast an evil spirit over me and had taken over my own will and replaced it with yours. Yesterday, when I announced my decision to sell my business, I fully expected that I would have to fight off a million objections. I assumed that you would not like this decision. So what was your response? You said that if I was not happy with my present situation I certainly should make a change. That was a very kind response, and I really appreciated it. Dad, I also had considerable difficulty in getting along with you. Most of the time, the problem was perfectly simple: I felt that you really hated me a lot. I, in turn, treated you in a defensive and hostile manner—often purposely goading you on until you got furious with me. My childhood recollections are of being beaten, yelled at, scolded for being stupid or slow, being told that I would be a failure when I grew up because I didn't like getting out of bed, etc. Certainly there were occasional happy moments, too, but the overall impression I clearly got was that you deeply hated me and wished me dead. I know that I made the worst of a very bad situation because I often did just those things which would cause you to become the most angry with me. Children have a way of doing strangely perverse things. Since you didn't love me, I was going to do everything I could to make your life miserable too. So we sadly spent our time making life miserable for each other.

In later life, I often caught myself doing things which I thought might cause you at least to respect me. I think that in a way, my efforts to make my business a financial success were partially because you would be pleased with this. In spite of the unfortunate relationship that you and I had when I was a child, I still secretly wanted you to like me. Again, I may have acted sarcastic and annoyingly egotistical when you were around (the old defense mechanism in action again) but all that I really wanted was your love. I think now that you, perhaps, also wanted things to be better. Sure, you would often be angry and critical, but that was just part of the ugly game that we were both playing.

But then I ran into hard times, and now with a perfect opportunity for you to really rub in the fact that I had been foolish in not running my business with the proper controls (and this, unfortunately is something you might have been inclined to do in past years) you instead offered me a loan on your life savings. That was an extremely kind thing to do. I realize that you would never have done it if you didn't secretly care for me, as I have secretly cared about you. In spite of the perfectly miserable way that both of us have treated each other for most of our lives, there was much more to the relationship than was apparent on the surface. With two sons of my own now, I have a very good idea how a father can feel about his children, and I can understand that you may have feelings that you have never been able to express to me.

There is an old saying that goes like this: "Today is the beginning of the rest of my life." What it means to me is that each day is a beginning, and it is never too late to try to make the quality of one's life just a bit better than before. In a few years I will turn 40, and both of you will be in your 80's. That's an awfully late age for a family to learn how to love each other, but it is never too late. I certainly don't expect any miracles to happen, but I feel that we have made a good beginning. Perhaps we will discover that gradually all of the anger and hurt can be replaced by consideration and affection. I am willing to try this, and now I think that you are too.

Love,
Dan

To this letter his mother replied:

Dear Dan,

Your letter means a great deal to me, for I have never stopped loving you or any of my sons. I feel certain that when you can settle your business affairs, you will again be happy and relaxed.

Thank goodness, I've overcome my aggressive attitude, for I don't think I realized how obnoxious it was. I guess it stemmed from the fact that I wanted everything to be perfect for you, but I now realize that everyone must work out their destiny in their own way.

Do let me know if there is anything I can do for you. You have a wonderful family and should look forward to much happiness when you sell the business.

My love to all,

Mother

To this, Dan's father added these lines:

We do seem to get along, even though we scrap occasionally. You have always been my favorite son, Dan, and I'm sorry you thought otherwise as a child and young man.

Love,
Dad

A year later, still working on the problem, Dan wrote to his parents:

Dear Mother and Dad,

I'm writing this very long letter in an attempt to explain as directly and honestly as I can just why it is that when we get together there is still often a lot of tension and hostility. It is important, to me at least, to set the record straight, and my hope is that you will read through what I have to say so that you will then understand why I respond as I do to both of you.

When we get together I see you in two ways:

1) I can observe you in the present and react to the things you now say and do in much the same way as a perfect stranger would respond if he were to meet you for the first time.

2) Also, to the extent that circumstances and conversations remind me of scenes out of my childhood, I can react to the memories of these past events—just as if they were taking place in the present.

When I am with either of you, I am reminded of past feelings. Why is this so important? Because practically all of these past feelings were ones of pain, fear, grief and

*anger! I want you both to know about the memories I
have of my childhood. This would serve to help you to
understand why I respond to you in the ways that I do
now in the present, and it would be of some satisfaction
to me to have told you such things as well.*

*My memories of the way things were when I was little
are that I was not held and loved in a tender way by
either of you. In fact, instead of the love that I craved, the
treatment that I received from both of you could best be
described as plain brutality.*

*Fights and arguments were a way of life in your mar-
riage long before I was born, so I suppose it was only
natural that such hostility would be directed towards me
virtually from the day that I was born. My defense against
this treatment was to become stubborn and negative myself. If I wasn't getting what I wanted (tender love) then,
by God, I wasn't going to give either of you what you
wanted. So my style became one of finding out what you
desired and then trying to do exactly the opposite.*

*Your response was to beat me. Mother, I can clearly
remember you saying to Dad when he got home from
work, "The boys have been bad today and need to be.
punished." This would happen often, and your response,
Dad, was to beat us with your belt. The more you hit us,
the angrier we got, and the angrier we became, the more
we tried to get even. Getting even consisted of being bad
kids. This vicious cycle progressed to the point where at
one time I can remember, Dad, that you were swinging
at Jim with the metal buckle end of the belt, and Mother
screamed lest you kill him!*

*As a boy, I would go through the day in a state of
mortal terror, wondering when the next attack would take
place. In addition to the physical beatings, there were
verbal assaults which were equally painful. From you,
Mother, this took place in the form of trying to manipulate me into doing something I didn't want to do. You
would push me for hours on end, trying in every way you
knew how to bend my spirit until I hardly knew what I*

*really wanted myself. The brain-washing administered by
the Chinese is child's play compared to such pressure from
you. You, Dad, would verbally attack me in the form of
"put-downs." You would say to me, "The reason why
you're going to be a failure when you grow up is because
you don't like to get out of bed in the morning. . . ." Or,
when I was trying to do some task and making the typical
mistakes that a child makes, you would snatch the work out
of my hands and say in disgust, "Can't you do anything
right?" The net result was that I felt afraid of punishment,
totally inferior as a person, deeply hurt, and finally . . .
boiling mad. I was too small, too weak, too ignorant to
fight back but I would have dreams of becoming a huge
beast and then tearing you both apart limb by limb, crush-
ing your bones into little pieces. The resentment I had
over the way that I was treated built into a tremendous
hate. Hate with a vengeance that could almost have made
me into a future murderer.*

*One thing saved me—Grandmother. She gave me the
love that I so badly needed and wanted. She treated me
with kindness and sensitivity. Life with her was pure joy.
It was thanks to her that I was able to understand that
there was an alternative to the misery I was experiencing
in my own family. Her love gave me hope.*

*Mother, I can hear your reply right now. It is, "But I
did love my sons. I gave them everything I had." I honestly believe that you do think that this is the case. To be
sure, you did take care of us. You did feed us, wait on us
like a servant, spend many hours reading to us or trying
to teach us things. You did tell us that you loved us, but
none of these acts can be a substitute for real love. I
am convinced that you don't know what love is. Real love
is the way that a mother like Grandmother holds a small
child, the way that she strokes him and looks into his eyes,
the way that she is there, soft and gentle, loving him with
all her heart and showing this in the tender way that she
treats him. Mothers who really love their children don't
use and abuse them like you did us. I know that from the*

bottom of my heart because, thank God, I did receive this love from Grandmother when I was a child, and later on I have experienced it again from my wife. Now, I feel it also for my own children, and Mother, I'm telling you I didn't receive one ounce of this kind of real love from you!

Ironically, Dad, in spite of the brutal beatings, in spite of the many times that you treated me as if I were a worthless piece of garbage, you did once in a while show that you were also capable of loving. I can remember one occasion in particular in which you rubbed ointment on a sunburn I had. You did this with great tenderness and genuine concern, and for a moment, it was as if a great spark of love was there. I know that you do understand what love really is because Grandmother was your own stepmother, and I sometimes wonder why you were not able to show any of this. Somehow, for some reason, the circumstances were such that virtually all of the time, the only emotions that you expressed towards me were anger and contempt.

By the time that we moved to Bromfield Street, the situation at home had already reached an impossible state. Jim responded by breaking into that house and smashing things. Stan used to cut himself all the time. I ran away from home. Why do you think we all did these things? By accident? We did them because each of us in his own confused way was trying to tell you how miserable we had become. When I ran away from home, I was saying that life in that household was simply unbearable. There was so much violence, hatred, unhappiness and insanity that even as a small child, I knew life had to be better elsewhere. I left with the dream that like in the story of Peter Pan, I would be able to find Never Never Land where I was treated with kindness and appreciation. So I went out into the woods, sat in a tree and hoped that a miracle would take place. As time went on, and I got colder and hungrier, I realized that there was no practical way of leaving home. I couldn't go to Grandmother's house because Dad was her step-son and she would certainly make me go back home. There was no one else who might take me in.

At this point, Dad would come looking for me, and would call out to me, "I know you're there, Dan," I responded by making a grunting sound in my throat. I did this on purpose. It was my way of saying, "Yes, I'm here and I know I have to go back to your house." My hope, Dad, as I sat in that tree grunting, was that you might possibly be pleased enough to have found me to be willing to listen to the reasons why I had run away from home. I climbed down from the tree, rehearsing in my mind the things I wanted to tell you, but before I got a chance to talk to you, you grabbed me and beat me so hard that I just gave up. From then on, I didn't bother to make any more attempts to communicate with you.

After we were forced to move, I started to fall apart. There seemed to be no way that I could escape all of the anger, brutality and misery that surrounded my life. No way, that is, but one. I could go crazy.

When you go crazy, your daydreams become more important than the events that actually take place around you. In that way, you don't have to suffer the pains of reality any longer. I could put up with the almost daily whippings from you, Mother (do you remember the whipping bush in the back yard and the way you would whip us with a stick every afternoon when your headaches got particularly bad?), and I hardly felt them at all. I could listen to the tirades of abuse from you, Dad, about not doing my homework (how can anyone do homework when he is crazy?), and about all of the other ways that you found me lacking, and just let the words roll off my back. Everything might be horrible in the real world, but all kinds of nice things happened to me in my day dreams!

Luckily, I was able to start psychiatric treatment before I went totally insane. Jim was not as fortunate. Through treatment, I was able to leave home, and finally to detach myself from the influence that both of you had upon me. I went on to have a happy, successful life, and to overcome the horrors of my childhood. However, when I do see either one of you now, admittedly rare though such occasions may be, I find that ancient feelings are once again brought up. To be sure, you no longer beat me, Dad, nor do you try to dominate my thoughts and feelings, Mother, but in spite of the changes in our present relationship, I am still reminded by words, expressions and gestures of past feelings that I had as a child. When this happens, my emotion is to want to torture both of you to death—in just the same ways that you so cruelly abused me when I was a small and helpless child.

I have some more explaining to do: First of all, my children (and all of my close friends) know exactly how I feel about my childhood and about both of you as parents. In fact, the two of you are about the only people who haven't been informed. Why has this been so? Because I had the notion that although the relationship between you and me was terrible for me as a child, it might improve as I got older. I thought that there might be a chance that some kind of positive friendship would develop. I now realize that this would have been impossible—so long as I was concealing from you how I felt about the way that you had treated me. From now on, I will try to be as honest as I can in expressing my true feelings.

However, you need not fear any harm. Although there is murder in my heart, there is also awareness in my head that you both have tried in later years to make up for some of the things you did. As I have grown older, I have been able to guess at some of the reasons why you treated your children so cruelly. With my own self-understanding has come an understanding of some of the terrible pressures each one of you must have endured as a child. I feel sure that the extent of your own suffering had to be at least as great as my own.

Our family troubles could most likely be traced back many generations. Intellectually, I am well aware that you did the best that you could under the circumstances. To be fair, I should not leave the impression that all of the experiences that I had with both of you as a child caused only pain and suffering . . . or that intense anger was the only *emotion I had. There were pleasant moments as well. I can particularly remember the thrill of going to Cape Cod, and being carried out into the waves and dunked into the water by you, Dad. I have very fond memories of being read the story of Kim, and of course the nightly lullabies that you both sang to us.*

The difficulty was that for every pleasant moment there were ten miserable ones. It was easily possible to express the joy of the happy times, but virtually forbidden to let out the anger caused by the unpleasant experiences. I can recall that whenever I did express any anger you would say, Mother, "I know what you need, Dan. When you're angry like that you need an enema." And so you would flush out my insides with hot water. I was left with the impression that getting angry was a "dirty" thing to do (since whenever I let out any hostilities, you insisted that I have an enema), and the result was that I bottled up my feelings of rage inside of me. The longer I held in such feelings, the more intense they became—until I carried around a virtual hydrogen bomb in my psyche. Now, after 39 years of holding it in, that bomb has been set free, and it is pointed directly at both of you!

So how shall we deal with this situation? Seven years ago I simply tried to eliminate all contact with you. This was an artificially rigid solution, and when you begged to see us again, I consented to occasional visits.

At that time, I tried a different approach. I made an attempt to try to forget the past and see what I could do to make those few times that we did get together in the present as happy as possible. That solution was also ab-surd. You can't forget the past, and no matter how hard I tried, my feelings came through anyway. *I was often sarcastic, bitter and critical. Obviously, in spite of my efforts to be "nice," I wasn't able to cover up my real feelings.*

The only solution that makes sense is just to be honest. That is what I will do whenever I see you, and I invite both of you to do the same. If you have angry thoughts

*to express towards me as well, then it would be good for
you to get them out also.*

*I want to end this letter on one final note: I am blessed
with a healthy body and a fine mind. I now live a life that
is filled with much happiness and satisfaction, and because
of this I am very glad to be alive. The simple fact is that
I would not exist if it were not for the two of you, and so
I can thank you both for bringing me into the world.*

Dan

Dan described to me what happened in reply to this
long letter:

*Today I received a large, heavy manila envelope from
my mother. It was quite bulky, as was my letter, and from
the outside it appeared to be an equally serious reply. Inside
the envelope were three brand new dish towels. No letter.
I know that this was my mother's attempt to make a response. She was saying, "I have received your letter, I
know that it would be good for me to send a reply, but I
am too confused to verbalize it." The exact meaning of the
three dish towels is not clear to me, but I understand that
this is the best she can do. My father did not reply directly
to me at all, but he did send each of my children a post
card. On it he wrote, "You must be going back to school
this week. I'm going to attend some lectures on being a
salesman, myself." At 75, he still works as an active
salesman. Whenever something happens that is upsetting
or confusing to him, he simply works harder. He understands his work, but he doesn't understand life.*

Dan also analyzed for me the three techniques that
he had used in his effort to communicate with his parents:

Isolation: *Realizing that they were not capable of being
the parents I had wanted and needed, that they could not love
me and communicate with me in ways that I wished, I
cut off all contact with them. My attitude was one of "let
them be just a past memory." This was an unsatisfactory
solution because it made a big issue out of our lack of*

relationship. They would try in every way they could to reestablish contact and I would have to work to avoid them. I discovered that the process of putting them off consumed too much time and energy.

Making the best of an unfortunate situation: *I have tried at some length just to "forget the past," and see if I couldn't deal with my parents as though they were just two old and sick persons who needed all of the help and affection I was capable of giving them. After all, they were only the product of their miserable environments. To see them as fellow sufferers rather than the individuals who caused me so much pain, and to be as nice as possible to them was a humane thing to do. Unfortunately, the trick didn't quite work. Like it or not, I discovered that ancient feelings of anger and fear would take place when I was with them. When I tried to overlook such feelings, it did terrible things to my psyche. My parents loved the kind of attention I gave them* (their *needs for love and affection are even greater than mine . . .), but I couldn't continue to be "nice" when I felt like hitting them with a stick.*

Honest confrontation: *This means that you decide simply to express your true feelings—whatever they may be—towards your parents in as open and direct a manner as possible. My experience has been that I feel most comfortable doing this, but that it leaves my parents in a state of shock. Their response is to: a) Pretend that I have said nothing and change the subject as soon as possible. b) Cry, become abusive, and act deranged. c) Make some kind of silly response. (Like sending me dish towels in the mail.)*

The problem of course is that the truth is so horrible that they simply cannot face it. "Did we really beat you with a stick when you were an infant, Dan? I seem to have forgotten what happened . . ." They have a way of remembering only the nice things that happened and forgetting the unpleasant scenes. They beg you not to bring up the past, not to express the feelings that you have about it, and they do so with good reason. No one likes being confronted with memories of situations they are later ashamed

*of. This is especially painful when it is one's own children
doing the accusing. I know that it would hurt me a lot
if my own kids did this to me!*

*My present intention is to continue to be honest with
my parents, but I am aware that this is a difficult thing to
do. To be truly honest, I would have to spend most of my
time telling them how angry I was.*

Dan puts into words the experience of many young
adults who can't seem to feel good about their parents. The
old grudges and angers are near the surface whenever they
get together. But either they don't dare reveal these feelings, or their parents can't hear them when they do. "All
we want is for you to be happy, you have absolutely no
reason to be unhappy. We always did what we thought was
best for you because we loved you," and so on. The
easiest way out of this is to create an isolation or near-
isolation. Many young people do just this; they visit their
parents only on major holidays; they don't talk about anything important; and when they find themselves getting
tense or enraged, they find an excuse for leaving.

Well do I remember my visits to my parents after I had
gone away to college. My father was always working, so
he remained as inaccessible as he had been when I was
a child. My mother lay depressed in her bedroom, burning into my soul her message that by leaving home I had
abandoned her to a miserable life. I lay in my own bedroom, burning with need and rage. I could not then dare
to tell her my feelings about her failing me as a mother
with anything approaching Dan's candor, so I avoided
real contact, said little, left early.

But I found that what Dan says about this noncon-
frontation technique is true—I kept getting invited home
and feeling guilty when I refused. As he says, ". . . putting
them off consumed too much time and energy." I would
add that carrying around lots of heavy feelings about important people in your life feels burdensome. You don't
feel free to enjoy other things.

Dan then describes his attempt to solve this problem by

trying to "forget the past." He tried to see them as "just two old and sick persons who needed all the help and affection I was capable of giving them." Many people use this technique. In fact, it is recommended by many parents, like Sally's mother in chapter 1. But as I found when I tried it, and as Dan finds too, "being nice" when you are angry is not only difficult, but you also end up feeling dishonest.

Dan then tried the hardest method of all: honest and direct confrontation with parents. He reported that this did not work in the sense that his parents could not respond in kind. Even if we find the meaning of the three dish towels to be, "Wash your own dirty dishes!" the reply did not satisfy an angry son, trying to force a confession of guilt and a plea for leniency.

Nevertheless, after confronting his parents with his feelings about them, Dan found that *he felt better inside himself*. Though his parents could not reply in any way that he could accept, he found that some of the burden of his old feelings was eased, and he could enjoy his personal life much more. This is the way Peter (chap. 5) felt after trying to engage both his parents in a direct exchange of feelings. Something inside says, "Well, I tried as hard as I could, and the failure of the attempt is not my fault." Though Dan intends to continue being totally honest with his parents, my guess is that he will not need to put so much energy into this as time goes on. He will probably feel better attending to his own life and not feel so much need to "make them see."

Feelings about parents can be resolved internally even when attempts to resolve them encounter-style do not work. When my own mother died shortly after an argument with me, I became deeply depressed. She had put me in an impossible position by insisting on visiting my wife and me just the day we were bringing our newborn twins home from the hospital. I replied that we could handle a visit much better on the day before, when she could see the babies in the hospital nursery, and while my wife was still getting help from the nurses. This was the way we wanted it, not the following day when we would be trying to cope with four children at home, two of them newborn twins. My mother was furious at having her plan rejected. I was furious at having our needs ignored. She hung up the telephone angrily, not seeing how she and my father could visit on the day I suggested. The next day she called back, agreeing completely with our proposal. I thanked her but she brushed it off, denying totally that she had wanted it any other way, or that she had been angry. When they did visit, she was in a fury, so tense with the effort of concealing anger that she could not enjoy the visit. The next day she had a stroke and died. My mother and I never had the chance to take up the subject of the argument or its importance in our relationship. I felt terribly punished for taking what I felt was a reasonable position on the issue, protecting my wife and myself from extra stress at a time when we could not have handled it. But internally I felt terribly guilty, like a murderer. And I carried the guilt feelings in the form of a depression for a long time. The turning point came when I found a way to express them, to discharge the terrible burden. It was therapy that gave me the setting in which I felt safe enough to do it. I had to resolve the feelings inside myself because my mother was not alive to work them out with me. Even if she had not died, I doubt if she would have been able to hear them.

My own experience adds to Dan's and Peter's. If your parents can't or won't hear your feelings, all you can do is try to express them. At least you don't end up feeling cowardly or hypocritical. The *trying* is important. It's not enough to suppress your feelings with the thought, however true, They'd never understand! If your parents won't see you as a person *separate* from their ways, you must still show them you *are* separate. Even if you do not prove it to them, you must prove it to yourself.

CHAPTER 7

I've come home again

The following story was written by a thirty-five-year-old woman who was in therapy with me while divorcing her husband.

This story starts a couple of years ago when I went home to tell my parents that my 14-year-old marriage was over. I explained that I felt my marriage had been over for about 7 years and that I was hanging in because of our two children and also because of a feeling that if things were wrong it was "my fault." I explained that I love my work. I'm an astrology teacher—a vaguely acceptable way of being a philosopher in our culture. I said I loved a married man who was not free to live with me—and who might never be free. I said that the time I had with this man I felt was so high—so special—so close and so deep that I would be his mistress forever if that were the only way I could be with him. I'd wait to marry him if that ever came about. I asked my parents for closeness—for the ability to listen—to understand and love and support me. I did not ask for money.

My parents and my brother were horrified. They said I needed psycho-analysis immediately, and that I was an unfit mother. They discussed (as if I were not there) "what to do with my children" as if I were no longer re-

sponsible for them. I was furious, and told them to "fuck off," but tried to keep the communication going. In fact, it was Yom Kippur, and although I had not been to temple for 15–20 years (I had married a Protestant, a WASP), I went to temple with my brother. Recently, I have been writing religious services with a colleague of mine and also using students, dancers and yogis to perform them. Our service is a total experience combining mind, body, emotions and involving the entire congregation in slow, hypnotic movements and real closeness with one another. So, there I am—a mystical far-out astrologer who sometimes practices meditation in Quaker meeting (if the vibes are right)—sitting with my brother in temple.

They were doing the Kol Nidre. "Forgive me, Father; for the sin of . . . for the sin of . . . for the sin of . . ."

And I'm thinking, Yep, yep, yep, I've done 'em all, and I start to laugh. And I really dig that Freud had to be a Jew—the guilt trip—the grief trip had to be his shtick. And I'm digging why Christ did his trip. Christ had to do something about the Kol Nidre, "Christ, let's do something," he said. So I'm laughing and my brother is horrified, and my parents are horrified. And I'm in love and I'm very high and when I'm with my man I remember a place, some knowledge, some love that's been so high, so much light, so much energy that nothing else I ever experienced in my thoughts or senses can touch that place in me.

A few months later my parents came to stay with my children while I went away for a weekend with my lover. The morning I left, I stood in the kitchen in my tie-dye jeans suit, and I'm packing this gross shopping bag full of tamari and sunflower seeds and corn oil and brown rice and salad stuff and teas. And my mother walks into the kitchen and she says, "You're going, with that bundle?! You look like my grandmother."

Then she laughs and holds my hand and says I look gorgeous. And my father takes me to the airport and he's really laughing over this yin-yang situation, this lovely lady with this gross bundle. And he's still laughing when

I thank him for the soft-shell crabs he bought for me to take back home after my last visit, and he's laughing about my lover's remark—"I wish there was someone I could tell that my lover gave me crabs!"

And I look at my father's face and he is smiling and having a contact high with me and being here and now. But, he's also my father, and deeply concerned for me and my children. And I dig it all—I'm high with him—I love him. And I'm sad, because I am a parent, too. I leave to get on the plane. "Bye, Papa." I feel so full of it—so close to him.

When I return, I find my mother with my kids. She explains she does not want to leave as soon as I get back, my father would not let her, because one of my kids who has been having problems and therapy was anxious while I was gone. My mother then explains what she did to handle the situation and I feel she has handled the children with amazing love and competence and tell her so. Then Mother says she will stay a few days just to be with me and I am glad, although I am well aware she wants to check me out. So, she stays, and watches me whip through my days dealing with my needy children, my classes and clients, cleaning, cooking and meeting with my lover. And she watches this gyroscopic whirlwind of activity, and things get done. She sees I'm busy, but I'm calm.

And the night before she leaves, she holds my hand and she says, "I just want you to know, I couldn't do what you do. It's exhausting and risky and scary. But I admire you, and support you completely."

My eyes fill, and I feel overwhelmed. I feel so close to her, so full of love. And I perceive from her the message as, "Go baby!" And I feel she has seen and accepted me and my life. I've come home again!

This dynamic young woman took a big risk. At the depth of her own despair over the end of her fourteen-year-old marriage, with two children to worry about, she went home and revealed to her family that she had given up the marriage, which felt loveless to her, and was now going to live alone, care for her children, and take her chances on a relationship with a man who could not guarantee her any future security. Most parents would break up over that one, and hers did. Amazement, shock and then anger and denunciation. And her counterreaction was rage and withdrawal. "I told them to fuck off!" She then demonstrated by making her own way on her chosen course that, whatever they might think of her decisions, she was clearly going to live them out. As another woman told me once, "If you let your parents see your doubts and hesitations, they'll take over your life and you'll have to do an adolescent rebellion number all over again. If you let them know you're definitely firm in your life-style, they may help or refuse to help, but you won't be usurped!"

And these were obviously loving parents who love each other. They soon saw that their headstrong daughter meant what she said and decided to offer whatever help they could. As time passed and it seemed more likely that her love relationship might possibly solidify into a second marriage, they felt better about being helpful and supportive to her and her children.

The first message of this example is clear. You *can* tell your parents what you're doing and why, if you feel resolved enough to stand firm should they violently disagree with you. If you do stand firm, they may very well end up helping you. Even if they never agree with your decisions, you can continue to talk to them about it all, and to make use of their ideas and advice whenever you choose.

Another message is that parents and their adult children can and do tell each other they are crazy and to fuck off without implying that they don't love each other. "I love you but I can't agree with what you're doing" is a perfectly valid message going from parent to child or the other way around. It amounts to a recognition by both parties of the differences in each other's chosen life-styles. As a child psychiatrist for the past twenty years, I must solemnly avow that more than half the grief taking place between parents and adolescent and young adult children is due to failure by both sides to make this vital distinction. We must face the fact that our values and patterns of living are changing so rapidly that dealing with the next generation, *older or younger, is a transcultural* interaction. We have to borrow a bit of detachment from the sociologist and the anthropologist and realize that we just don't know enough about the internal programming of our parents, or about the peer pressures upon our grown-up kids, to judge what they want to do, or even what they want *us* to do. Early anthropologists not only observed but *judged* the cultures they found and studied. Comments like "civilized" and "uncivilized" were found in "scientific" papers. We're past that now. We can admit that we can't see other people's worlds from the inside. Nowadays we must also realize that neither parents nor their grown-up children can see each others' worlds from the inside, either. Parents tend to keep on judging their children's decisions long after the children have become adults. That's understandable. Parents were for so long the Gods; everything was decided upon, everything appraised by them. Reward and punishment, the weapons of the parent, are hard to put away when the parent-child time ends and the *person-to-person* time must begin.

When your grown children tell you to fuck off after you've given them the same kind of honest reaction you gave when they came home at 5:00 A.M. from a party at age fourteen, it's hard to take. This mother and father were honestly frightened by their daughter's risky and impulsive-looking decision to stake her future on a relationship that might never solidify. They probably have had a hard enough time accepting her astrology career. But somewhere inside themselves they found the objectivity to remember—"At thirty-five, she's an adult. It's her life, not ours. We can choose to help her or not, but we can't stop her. And whatever she does, we love her."

Another message comes through here. Sally's mother and Billy's mother come across like total strangers to their children when they give advice. As Sally wrote to her mother, "Most of what you write about me could be written just as meaningfully about anyone in the world!" Advice or feedback given to a child when he or she asks for help or tells parents about a life decision needs to be *personal* response. *"I,* Herb or Marge or Jack or Isabel, tell *you,* my son Henry or Peter or my daughter Sally or Janet, what I think and feel as a *person.* Here are my life experiences and their outcomes, which make me feel whatever I feel about *your* life experiences." When parental advice could have come from a newspaper column, it is generally useless. Why should I accept advice from someone who doesn't know who I am?

These examples also say something about what should happen during adolescence. When adolescents are figuring out who they are, in the world larger than home, parents must observe and react to the person the child is becoming If parents don't show they know who the adolescent is, he or she will not feel like incorporating their advice, however wise, later on. The adolescent, in turn, needs to be bold enough to let parents know who he or she really is, to give parents *honest* readings of mood, goals and values. The sly adolescent who hides his or her real thoughts and feelings from "them" to avoid hassles ends up in worse trouble later when "they" can't recognize the person who is their child.

This all leads to the conclusion that many adolescents and young adults would rather not see—when you decide who you are and therefore what you will do in your life, you have assumed the responsibility for what happens to you. "They" are no longer at fault. "It's my life," said one young person to me, "I eat my cake, then clean up my own crumbs."

PART THREE

Trying to find my parents

CHAPTER 8

Interviews with young adults

As I work in psychotherapy with young people, I come across the same issue over and over: a powerful need to go home, to force an encounter with parents. There is a desire to "say all the things that are important between us and then see if we can like each other or not. It feels as though some old issue needs to be settled."

Whether the parents are loved or hated or loved *and* hated, whether the young adult looks forward to a warm welcome or dreads the very sight of his or her parents, many of these young people feel propelled toward revisiting their old guides and judges. Especially now, when values and behavior codes are changing at such an exponential rate in American society, young adults who have been away long enough to have an inkling of who they are becoming need to go back home and try to relate this firmer new self to their mother and father.

Some of these attempts are terribly painful because childhood was painful, as with Henry and Peter, or because parents have been unable to understand the new conditions under which young people live. Painful because communication in many families has been so poor that young people and parents are totally unprepared to hear how their relationship was felt and remembered by the other. Billy's mother said it:

"You have absolutely no reason to be unhappy . . . Your father and I always put you . . . ahead of ourselves!" Emily's father couldn't listen: "Stop thinking of yesterday . . . live for today and tomorrow!"

If you look at your own life, you can see that coming to terms with past relationships in your family is necessary not only for disturbed young people or psychiatric patients, but is important for *everybody*. This society is changing so fast that reconnecting our roots to the old (postcognitive) world of Mommy, Daddy, and me is something we all need to do.

While checking out the question, "Is it generally important for young people today to remain in touch with their parents?" I realized that if I limited my research to my patients I would not see how this issue is dealt with by young people who are *nobody's* patients, just normal individuals trying to shape an adult identity. So I found a researcher who interviewed young people on this issue, designing and carrying out her own interviews. I saw only the typed results. Many of the people she selected are unknown to me. None of their names was given to me.

When I first read these interviews, I was surprised to find that in most cases these young people had not dared to try direct *verbal* confrontation with their parents. Much more often, strong feelings were played out in action; just as commonly the responses were acted out as well. When a parent or grown child opened up an honest communication, more often than not this attempt was spurned. Sometimes it was recognized, but still not reciprocated in kind.

Nevertheless, these interviews give fascinating pictures of how articulate, intelligent and sophisticated young adults look at their parents' lives and at their relationships with them. I have decided to present the most interesting and revealing parts, in the hope that readers who are young adults or parents will feel the familiarity of these situations and consider with me how some of these painful dilemmas can be resolved in a better way.

As you read these interviews, bear in mind that they are the personal accounts of young adults—no longer living at home, mostly making their own lives, not children anymore. They are in their twenties and early thirties, not as old as many of us are when we begin to understand the mysteries of our parents' lives and to "forgive" them the sins of neglect or narrow-mindedness or missed opportunities for guidance which we feel they have committed against us. And bear in mind, too, that on the other side of the communications gulf, parents are worrying about what to do, how to help, how to understand what their children are feeling, believing and becoming. There is no one to *blame* for the lack of rapport, no culprit. The tragedy is the missed opportunity for *shared* feelings and the closeness that comes from understanding and accepting each other.

Many of these interviews show some closeness in the first twenty years, some shared feelings. But for young people then to lose their parents as friends and guides by the time adolescence ends seems from these interviews to be almost inevitable; certainly those who by the age of thirty report rapport of any depth with parents are in the minority. Something is lost. Parents, too, suffer a loss. It is not easy to love and feed and come to know a child and then have him or her leave your life without having become your friend. After listening first to young people, then to parents, we will try to show how there can be a better way.

1. "If you let this one get away, you are crazy."

A twenty-nine-year-old man, holder of a master's degree and planning to get a Ph.D. in clinical psychology:

I experience my parents (mother and stepfather) as basically open if I assert where and who I am. There has been a radical change around "work" and the way my parents perceive me. They have very strong notions of what is and what is not successful. What they are able to under-

stand is a business setting and being financially well off—certainly not leading a life of deprivation.

I am not formally working right now; I am preparing to be a therapist (applying to school, learning skills, learning about myself and so on). Therapy is totally alien to my parents. I have connected more with my mother in the past, but right now I don't want her in my life in any significant way—she has been altogether too much in it in the past. I limit my interaction with her to reassuring her that everything will be all right. She is afraid that I might not be able to take care of myself, that the new places I am going will be anxiety-producing enough that I might crumble. I resent that; I feel that I am approaching therapy with the perspective of being a professional.

I actually share very little with my stepfather at this point. I remember one phone conversation in particular. There was a job opening at a psychiatric hospital, and in the course of our conversation, he said that I was indulging myself, that I had no right to do so (just because "You've never discovered who you are!"), and the whole field of therapy was bullshit. He was very angry, but I think the source of it was an anguish he feels that I am so different from him, so foreign to him. The thing that really got me, though, was when he said, "It is your responsibility to solve the economic problems of the world." (!!!) MY RESPONSIBILITY!! Fuck you, I have no responsibilities of the sort! Furthermore, he doesn't solve any problems of that kind either. He is a parasite on the business community—he just makes money and plays around in it—he makes no contribution to society. My response to him is a giant "I don't want to!" When I asserted that, he backed down and I felt guilty that I had hurt him, but that is his problem. He is a very anguished man—he took over another man's family after having spent many many years taking care of his own mother (I don't believe he has ever been free of her)—he has, in fact, never been free to explore himself. I think way down he is very very angry about that. I also think he had very strong needs for me to be his son, and certainly the reverse is true. Unfortunately, much of our relationship was based on ritual. A good deal of what he said to me over the years has gone in one ear and out the other. I have always had to relate to him on his terms, and I really resent this. He doesn't even know me, and at this point, I cannot tell him who I am. To do so would entail a process of uncovering how we have failed one another, and I haven't the energy to do this now. I need it myself. Someday it will be important so that we are able to open up to new territory, but not now.

Clearly, I am not making this radical vocational change for them. It is definitely for myself. I hate going home, it makes me feel like a child. I don't want to have to "explain myself." I will go to the extent of reassuring them I am all right, and that I am going to be (am!) quite happy, and they will just have to trust that. I know what I am doing. I am not a child or a fool. It's my Goddamn life.

My mother, I think, is well aware of the impact she has on me. She is finally beginning to step back some. She is active, energetic and somewhat intrusive. She is very critical if she feels someone is going down the "wrong path." However, she looks at the superficial signs. My brother has long hair, and she gets on him for it. Yet she doesn't seem to notice his good qualities; his warmth, his humor, his generosity. She sees his long hair. Several years ago the family had a party where everyone invited their peers. Friends of my brother's came, and they had long hair and short skirts. "Who are those people, Alan?" He got quite angry and said she had no right to criticize her children's friends like that. She cowed, and I was happy to see it because I felt he spoke for all of us. If my friends are an issue for her, she makes them an issue for me. (I don't allow it anymore.) My mother is manipulative and decisive in the absence of a stronger force. My way of manipulating back was to say, see if I care, I will resent it. Then, if (or when) I failed I could turn the responsibility back over to her: "It was your idea, not mine."

There is one incident that really stands out for me. I had brought Jan, the woman I was seeing, home with me.

She and my mother hit it off tremendously—they are both active, dynamic, aggressive. There began a strong sense of sisterhood. It was Thanksgiving, and I was at the top of the stairs. My mother had her arm around Jan's shoulders. "Well, son, if you let this one get away, you are crazy." I was wildly upset. The impact that statement had on me was that I no longer felt I had a choice of whether or not I would marry this particular woman—one of the most important decisions of my life! I felt it was an incredible robbery. I felt teamed up against. When I tried to explain my feelings later to Jan, she simply didn't understand, was very hurt by me, felt I had attacked her for what she thought was a friendly gesture. I reacted with a great deal of guilt, was afraid I had killed our love. I spent an entire day in the worst anxiety attack I have ever had. I wept all the way to school in the car; I was physically ill with anxiety. I couldn't get warm.

Another theme which haunts me about my mother is my fear she didn't love my father. In fact, she might not have. She once told me it might have been a good thing he died when he did because he might not have been "successful." Again, success being based on work. My father was generous, funny and very loving. I have never been able to confront her about her feelings, nor myself with mine. Sometimes I think I am out to get my mother for not loving my father. The way I am currently dealing with my mother is to force her to keep her concerns to herself; I tell her not to waste her time worrying about me. Yet recently we had a phone conversation where she was very distant, and I know she was trying to step back, which is a good thing. But I suddenly was overwhelmed with a panic that I can't go home anymore. There was a momentary strong sense of loss.

This young man has been able to be very direct with his stepfather, for example, when he refused to accept his challenge to accept responsibility for the "economic problems of the world." He has taken clear charge of the selection of his career and will not accept dictation in this area. He is also able to look at his stepfather's problems and to guess at his struggle to fill the role of father in the family. However, the stepson is not willing to open up a more dangerous issue, "how we have failed one another."

Another serious communications barrier in this family, probably the most important one, is between the young man and his powerful mother. When she puts her blessing upon his girlfriend, he reacts with panic, right up from the toenails. "I no longer felt I had a choice of whether or not I would marry this particular woman—one of the most important decisions of my life!" He still needs to wall his mother off from any closeness to his male life-decisions, and he knows it because *she has been altogether too much in it in the past.*" It might well be that the time between fathers, when she was the only parent for him, gave her so much emotional control over him that he felt deep doubt over his ability to become a man away from his mother, augmenting the inevitable problems a young man always has in leaving the first love of his life. It would probably have helped if his mother had made clear the deepest mystery of his early childhood: how she felt about his real father. He has a grudge against her for seeming not to have loved his father.

Were I to design an ideal communication plan for this family, I would place on the agenda:

The mother should tell her son more about her real feelings toward his own father and her reasons for these feelings. If she loved him deeply, her son will feel reassured. If not, he is old enough to understand her reasons, *if they are truly expressed.* Here I am recommending a cocognitive style, sharing deep feelings with one's grownup child, just as this young man's mother wishes he could do with her, setting up the pattern of sharing *as equals.* In place of "Mother knows best, and you are not ready to do this," we have, "We are both people, and people have basically the same feelings regardless of age or relationship."

In the same way, this man should let his mother know how good his memories of his father are, and how it upsets him to hear her cast doubts on his goodness and on her love for him. This young man needs also to let his mother know how deeply tied to her he still feels, for example how he felt when she told him not to let Jan "get away." In talking to her about this, he'll become more aware of his oversensitivity to whatever she says or does, which is a pretty common thing for a son whose mother has been the only constant parent in his life. It he can realize this, he can then make allowances for his oversensitivity to his mother and she, being alerted, can understand her influence upon him and shape her behavior accordingly.

Of course, letting each other in on such deep feelings seems risky to both mother and son. But the alternative is something like Sally's situation with her mother—an endless game of reaching and rebuffing, defending against each other. For this son, there seems to be much energy tied up in defense against his mother's power over him, dating from far back. This energy could be liberated by an attempt at communication. Perhaps, as with Peter, he could feel unburdened even if Mother could not level with him. And if she could, they could resolve the tension between them.

2. "You pay dues in loneliness."

A twenty-nine-year-old woman, college graduate, who teaches social studies in a high school:

I do and I don't communicate with my parents. I hold a number of "radical" political and social views about our culture which my parents disagree with strongly. Yet, on many issues—like honesty, responsibility, doing good work, being loving—we agree. In fact, I respect very deeply what they have shown and taught me about those "virtues."

I am a socialist and a feminist (to use current jargon; I won't go into my particular interpretation of these two movements, but I am not an extremist in either case), and I think a great deal about our world and time. I have strong dreams that pertain to my beliefs, that people should share resources, that they should uncover their common needs and help one another in concrete ways, that we should overcome the fragmentation between us. I believe in communal living, though not sexually (I am a monogamous person). My father is a businessman (with IBM) and believes in "The American Dream." When I was in school and financially dependent on my parents, we got into terrific hassles because I was an activist and also pretty fanatical. They felt all my energy and rebellion as a personal denial of them, and I guess I felt that too, now that I think about it. I really was disgusted with them and their phony way of life. I wanted to experience everything I could, read everything I could, feel everything I could, and make up my own mind about what is right and what I wanted to be. I often felt humiliated by their lack of acknowledgment of me and my strengths—wow, I just plugged into how angry I used to get, and to their indifference to my struggles. It has been a long time since I have looked to them for a real exchange about living in the highest sense—about being a historical person—no wonder I have forgotten how frustrated and painfully angry I was so much of the time.

It is only recently that I feel they realize I am intelligent and a person with thoughtful ways of being. I used to go to great lengths to explain and share what I was doing and thinking—once I sent my mother some short papers on radical Christian theology, really beautiful statements, and her only response was that she preferred the essence of simplicity. That was in fact the last time I did that. It wasn't long after that I made my strongest break from them.

There was a law at my college that no undergraduate could live off campus until they were twenty-three or had their parents' permission. I wanted to move in with two friends; I hated the dorms beyond description. I wanted my own home, my own kitchen, my own everything. Naturally, my parents said no. (I think they were worried about my virginal soul—and well they might have . . . I

*had my first love affair about two months later, yea!!!)
So I told them I was going to be twenty-one in three
weeks—over semester break—and if they would not give
me permission, I was going to drop out of school again
and work, go to school at night. I still don't know where
I got the guts to do that—I certainly didn't want to drop
out of school at all. They were furious, more that I could
threaten them successfully than that I was going to move
off campus. At any rate, they did finally give permission.
All this was done over the phone, though there were in-
terminable discussions that vacation after the call. That
was a good time in my life, a very happy time, one that
I am only now beginning to have again. I knew enough
to be relatively free then, and to enjoy myself, but then
I hadn't come up against the blackness and weakness of
spirit I have since found in me. Let's see, it has been eight
years. In a way I think that I am breaking away again
from them, as I was then, only now it is them mired inside
myself. This is the first time I have considered it just this
way, pretty interesting.*

*There were more little times breaking with them. Choos-
ing to spend Christmas with a friend, rather than going
home as usual. I felt very guilty for a long time, so much
so that I didn't really enjoy myself. What made it all so
awful was that we never talked straight out about how
we felt over these incidents. In fact, it wasn't until I had
a year of therapy that I began to be direct and to make
them be direct back. We discovered a lot of projection of
feeling on both sides, and even more misunderstanding of
motives. What I often would experience as intrusion and
attempts at control was their trying to help me. They both
said in several ways, after we began talking, that they
agonized at how little happiness I seemed to have, that I
seemed frantic and deeply troubled. Their "telling me what
to do" (things like eat and sleep better and regularly, not
to rush around so much, to organize my money, stop seeing a particular man) were attempts to alleviate the crush
in my life. What made it so hard for us to communicate
is that neither they or I ever mentioned openly that I was*

perfectly miserable, seemingly for no good reason. They even suggested "professional help" which I refused. I am certain I didn't really know myself how desperate I was becoming, and I resented their intrusions terribly. Fortunately, I was exposed to people my own age who were "doing groups," and I finally began to see how important and good therapy would be for me.

I don't tell them about my relationships with men in detail; we don't talk about politics. Yet, I find that they have a wealth of knowledge about the world, and I am curious. So we talk about business, about investing money, about recipes, about photography. For emotional problems and help I go to my friends; for practice and worldly help I ask them. I now feel secure in my own life, and I'm sure they feel it, too, and are happy not to have the responsibility. As for new techniques, I do think the major help has been my growing ability to be honest and not ashamed of my feelings, and not to feel intimidated by theirs.

This young woman has split from her parents' political and social values in many ways, yet she sees how many of her basic beliefs are derived from theirs: "honesty, responsibility, doing good work, being loving . . ." She has gone through the typical hassles of the radical adolescent with "The American Dream" parents. But what interests me here is how, even though her differences and struggles for individuation have taken place vigorously, even desperately (note the guerrilla tactics around the issue of moving out of the college dorm), this young woman seems to retain a respect for her parents and their basic goodness.

I feel this is an important point. When the basic family relationships have been close and secure, they can survive many of the polarizations of adolescence and the value clashes of the generation gap. Apparently, there was a time when the parents felt her energy and rebellion as a personal denial of *them* . . . "I really *was* disgusted with them and their phony way of life." And Mother did miss an opportunity to get across some basic communication of her continued love and respect for her daughter on the occasion of the exchange of views on "radical Christian theology." Mother and Father missed another chance to share in her identity formation when they were so sticky about the move out of the dormitory. The move, and perhaps the victory in the battle that led to the move, resulted in "a good time in my life."

Another point emerging here is that breaking away from parents' beliefs has a cost: "You pay dues in loneliness for your independence," one young man said. Now the daughter senses that she is reliving the break internally. "I am breaking away again from them, as I was then, *only now it is them mired inside myself.*" Hurting parents' feelings brings guilt feelings, like "choosing to spend Christmas with a friend, rather than going home, as usual." In the same way, parents feel guilty when they feel they have failed to meet the needs of a child. The real cost, however, lies in lack of communication. *"What made it all so awful was that we never talked straight out about how we felt."* After therapy, when the young woman led her family into openness, they saw what they had been missing. *"We discovered a lot of projection of feeling on both sides, and even more misunderstanding of motives."*

That says it—you can't *know* what others feel unless they tell you. A family that can talk about their feelings when an adolescent breaks away might avoid some of the pain and the polarization.

3. "Love me as a separate person."

A twenty-six-year-old woman, college graduate, who makes architectural models:

I experience my parents as closed to me. We cannot talk about anything inside ourselves—not real feelings, that is. We always limit ourselves to subjects outside ourselves, and if we don't, there are problems.

One of the big events of my relationship with my parents came about five years ago when I wanted to get married. My mother had found out my boyfriend and I slept together and she called me a prostitute and said my clothes were cheap-looking. Later when I told them we were getting married, there was a blanket of silence. When all four parents got together to set a date, my mother refused to give her consent, saying we were too young. She said there had to be a trial period and that we had to be nice to the families and to be helpful around home. After a week she came around. I think she was jealous about my going away from her. (Later, after my husband and I had split up, I told my mother she was right, that we were too young, but she didn't say anything, and now we don't discuss it.)

The other things we can talk about are school (my mother is interested in "education"), and she respects my artistic ability. My father always wants to know what I am doing for work, about my roommates, about the actualities of my life, but not what is going on inside.

My parents are closed emotionally (they are liberals on the outside), and I feel a lot of anger at that from the past. I am unable to ask them to love me. I sometimes feel a deep and infantile need because my mother has never given in those ways; she is very uptight. My father is as well. Whenever I have reached out in crucial times, I have felt rejected by them.

Another terribly important event for me was somewhat over a year ago when I attempted suicide and went to a hospital. I was weak, hallucinating, had no friends . . . and my parents were really horrible. I told them I wanted to go to the hospital and they used every argument they could think of against it. They felt my therapist was wrong, that the hospital was evil—they didn't want me in a hospital at all because they wanted to think everything was fine. Finally they said they wouldn't give me the money for it, and I told them I was going anyway, and that I would borrow money if I had to. They got hys-

terical and chased after my therapist until he got away
from them. (I don't have anything more to do with them,
financially.)

They also try controlling me in sneaky ways. They are
supercareful because I am a "mental patient." They call
up my social worker or my therapist to ask, "how is she?"
They are always dissatisfied. I have a part-time job because
I'm still in intensive therapy and I can't really handle
more work. My mother says, "Oh, ick." When I told them
I was going to do some volunteer teaching, she told me I
ought to be earning money.

Now, when they do give we warm feelings, I withdraw
because I don't trust it; I know it will be followed by a
control attempt. I try to stay emotionally uninvolved: I
don't show my feelings much, I act like a good little girl,
am polite, am role-playing all the time. I try to be elusive.
All this keeps me from getting caught.

My parents have a certain idealistic ideology: they believe in environmental planning for the whole world;
everything should fit, and everything should be under control. I, on the other hand, demand freedom for my emotions—and I don't fit into their world. I really never do
know what will happen, and I want to learn to trust that
things will work because I trust myself and my emotions.
I don't want to be caught up inside, and I don't want my
world predictable. It takes a lot of strength to accept new
things and integrate them. I don't believe in a total con-
ception of perfection as they do. I want to discover the
world as it is, not make it something perfectly organized.

My parents think therapy is weakness. I fight their con-
ceptions of me by being a rebel, or splitting people into
good guys and bad guys. The good guys are like me (of
course . . .) and the bad guys are like them—phony, mean,
angry, malicious, out to take advantage of the good guys,
and destructive.

Other than the times I've mentioned, there haven't been
any real blowups, and none that have led to much im-
provement. It has been a gradual separation. As I become
more complete, they can sense it, but I have not been to-

*gether enough at any one point to say, "Here it is, I'm
a person," no self to say, "I'm me."*

*I am vulnerable professionally and artistically because
I can't use the talent that I do have. I think I am able to
have a good understanding of people. I can tell whether
what they are saying or doing is healthy. I'm perceptive,
not so up in the clouds as I was. I'm not as perceptive
about myself, but I'm learning. My parents just want me to
be successful on the surface. They aren't even aware of the
importance of being successful inside.*

*In order to deal with them better, I make an effort to
tell them what I am doing before they call my social
worker. I make things more explicit. I can tell now
more when the controls start coming in, and I can change
the subject or present things in such a way as not to
allow controls. I keep communication open on little things
and demand my independence. They now call me before
dropping in, for example. I want them to support me for
who I am and what I want to become, to love me as a
separate and independent person. Either they have an
image of me or maybe are disappointed and have given
up hope, I don't know, but I'm not convinced they will
be able to see me as me.*

Compare this situation with the one before. Where that
family could survive the polarization of the values, clashes
of adolescent versus parent, this one is not surviving. Here
we see separation, not with mutual understanding and respect, but through walling off, caution, guarded self-
protection. Probably most of this is due to a lack of
genuine gut-level closeness when the daughter was younger.
"I sometimes feel a deep and infantile need *because my
mother has never given in those ways.* She is very uptight."
Here I must stress that this is the daughter talking, and she
is very hurt and very angry. This not to say that Mother
did not try as hard as she could. Her failure to reach her
daughter deeply and movingly may have come from her
own inner limitations; perhaps she had a poor example of
this from her own parents. Or, perhaps, her daughter

turned out to be a genetic and constitutional combination of traits that baffled and turned Mother off from day one. The work of some psychiatrists, notably Stella Chess, suggests that infants display inherited constitutional traits of "character" from the very beginning of life; their styles of dealing with people or new stimuli, their rhythms of feeding, activity and sleeping. Sometimes infants and mother as two kinds of creatures simply can't mesh. In this kind of situation battles develop and no one feels close or understood. But investigating why this hurt daughter couldn't trust her mother is the province of a case history in child psychiatry.

What is relevant here is that any chance for mutual affirmation and respect between these parents and this daughter as people is lost because of the inability of the parents to respect their daughter as a *separate person*. They don't trust her to be *herself*. Family therapy for all *might* get some channels open, but no one seems willing. This situation seems beyond repair.

Many otherwise functioning families fall apart because they cannot see and relate to each other's *separateness*. When parents can love a child only for doing what *they* would do in a situation, they are loving themselves and their own style more than they are loving their child. Children who have been loved in this way don't feel loved, they don't even feel *known*. This is why so many young adults report in these interviews, "My parents don't even *know* me!"

This interview reveals the daughter's almost paranoid rejection of any feelings or actions of her parents, suspecting "control moves." It is not that all these parents do is to try to control her, it is actually simpler than that. They (like millions of other parents of "normal" families), just can't trust anything of hers that is not their own idea, their own way of doing things. The only way a child can get loose from this subtle domination is to *tear* herself loose with deep suspicion and anger.

This is a central and vital issue in the normal stage of development from adolescent to young adult. If the family

has not helped you define who you are, you've got to do
it yourself, even against parental resistance. More on this
in the final chapters.

4. "If I have kids I am going to be around to help them grow up and discover who they are."

A twenty-four-year-old man, working toward his
Ph.D. in art history:

Jesus, where to begin. Did you see Murmur of the
Heart? *Well, my relationship with my mother was similar
to that. I was the youngest and her favorite. We were
together almost all of the time. When I was fifteen, I was
sent to prep school which was disastrous. For two years it
was a constant battle between the school and my parents
as to whether they would throw me out. I guess I don't
have to say that it was pretty rough on me: I was convinced that I was evil. No, really, I began to suspect that
I was the personification of evil because no one anywhere
wanted me around. My father I could understand; he had
never paid much attention to me except to criticize and
punish. Also, he was away on business more than half
the time. The school I could understand. I was rowdy,
didn't do well in classes and fought with the other boys.
I was always doing things I knew were against the rules,
on purpose. (Now I understand why, of course: I was full
of conflict and anger and sexual longing and confusions.
I had no one to talk to, no one to tell me these were
normal feelings. . . .) But my mother deserting me was
incomprehensible.*

*I did finally find out why, or rather, found out one
reason, and this was the beginning of everything for me.
Five of us from school took an illegal trip to New York
City, saying we were going home. Of course, we were
after booze and sex (we got the first). While we were
there, I saw, or thought I saw, my mother coming out of a
bookstore in the Village with someone's arm around her
shoulder, a man I didn't know and had never seen. She*

*has never admitted to it, so to this day I don't know for
sure if I really did see her. But there was something so.
right and so fitting about it. I suddenly put together that
my mother was having an affair with this man and wanted
to hide it from me, from all of us, of course.*

*I didn't go back to school; I stayed in New York. I
didn't care at that point what anyone did to me: I was
even too angry and numb to commit suicide. For about
two weeks no one knew where I was. I had enough money
to eat, of course, and I sponged a place to sleep off this
waitress I met. She is still a friend of mine, a real nut
she is. One afternoon the New York police came up to
me (I was in this restaurant) and said, "Your mother would
like to talk to you." I'll never forget that moment. I told
them to tell that whore that I didn't want to talk to her.
They were a little surprised, but with some persuading
(and I must admit that by this time all I needed was a
little), they got me to go with them. I talked to her on
the phone, and then my father, and was really very surprised myself at how worried they sounded. I think I did
distress them quite a bit those two weeks.*

*I got home, finally, and we had some pretty long con-
ferences, but, interestingly, they asked me what I wanted.
They suggested I see someone "professional" which I got
extremely defensive about. Finally, we decided that I
would go to our place in Pennsylvania for the summer. I
could be there by myself, or with some of my cousins, if
they came up for the weekend, but, essentially, it was to
be mine. I would have the summer to decide what I
wanted to do, though they told me I had to make some
choice or other. Let me see, I could go back to school,
and then to college: I could go to work, or I could go into
the army; whatever I chose would be okay, but they would
only give me money for school or for a shrink if I wanted;
they wouldn't support me doing nothing after the summer.
Now that I look back on that time I don't know how on
earth they could have hit upon such a good plan. That
summer was really fine: I met a girl and got my rocks off
regularly. I even began to really like her by the end of*

*the summer. I met a lot of kids who were into something—
going to school or working, doing something on their
own. I was impressed. Also, I knew I was smart (my one
saving grace; I still don't know how I learned that about
myself), so that even when I felt I couldn't do anything
or be anything, secretly I was certain I had something of
my own. By the end of the summer I had decided to go see
a therapist (a lot of kids had been very positive about
their experiences), and I was astonished at how explainable
everything was to me. I ended up going back to school—
the only college I could get into was a junior college because my record was so bad. But that was okay, too; I
needed to get started slowly.*

*One thing I will tell you right now: if I have kids (and
I do want to), I am going to be around to help them grow
up and discover who they are. I don't feel much besides
anger and blankness about my father. I don't even respect
him much, despite his "success." My feelings about my
mother are painfully mixed: she was much too close for
what is right for a boy child—it could have screwed me up
very badly: it has in lots of ways. But I want my life to be
more direct and more quiet, and my woman is going to
be mine.*

This young man's parents read the signals wisely when
he ran away to New York. Understanding that he needed
some decision-making space, they made the summer place
in Pennsylvania available to him. He could "be there by
myself . . . essentially, it was to be *mine.* I would have
the summer to decide what I wanted to do, though they
told me I *had* to make some choice." So often, when an
adolescent feels unable to understand his or her own distress or to trust parents to understand, acting out the
anger and pain and depression is the means of attempting
to communicate. This boy was saying, "I hate school, but
I don't feel I can trust you, my parents, to understand
my distress and loneliness. I feel deserted by Mother, being
forced to stay away at school. How could you do this to
me? I won't put up with it!" Then, seeing his mother with

her presumed lover causes the anger to erupt: "That whore!" But underneath, the needs for *understanding and firm, reasonable limit-setting* were there, and the parents' propositions made it clear to him that they understood those needs. "Now that I look back . . . I don't know how on earth they could have hit upon such a good plan." Fortified and feeling secure in the new deal with his parents, he can resume his growth toward an identity as an adult. That summer was a major turning point.

Too often, an acted-out cry for attention is so severe— a major criminal offense, actual addiction to a drug, pregnancy and refusal of an abortion—that the consequences of the acted-out call for help overshadow the original needs for help, and the future life of the adolescent may be bent permanently in a direction toward which it need never have gone. Not to say that a lifelong struggle against heroin addiction does not produce an identity that can be deep and real and of value to others in the world. Or that one cannot grow from the experience of having and caring for an unwanted child at fifteen. But the treasure of adolescence is in the *potentialities* of the young person. This does NOT mean merely academic potential, but that magical blend of talents and vital interests that flower during the teens and the special ways in which healthy adolescents find and develop these interests into lifelong patterns of love and work and creativity, patterns absolutely unique to each person.

When an adolescent feels too out of touch with parents to dare to approach them with despair—like Billy early in this book—when he knows Mom will say, "But you have nothing to be unhappy about!" he must turn then to an indirect way of expressing his dilemma. A hundred acid trips have consequences—one's head won't work well afterward for a long long time. In this way, too often, the original problem is compounded. This is why communication of *bad feelings* must be able to happen in a family. Any family can cope with good report cards, admission into the right college, getting a good job, and "Mommy, I love you." But too few can admit that despair and rage exist in all of us at times. Parents cut these communications off because they feel automatically at fault. If my wife says to me, "I'm very unhappy," and begins to weep, it is certainly less risky to shut her off with a quickly found surface explanation. After all, if she tells me what it is really about, I might turn out to have failed her in some important way.

Many parents can't bear the idea that unhappiness, particularly among adolescents, is normal and usual. These parents feel unable to cope with the great responsibilities of parenthood in the nuclear family, where two adults have to know *everything* and fix *everything*. So the commonest way of avoiding that feeling of "my child is in despair—how have *I* failed?" is to overlook the despair until it reaches epic proportions: the common pattern is that the father retreats into his work—"he had never paid much attention to me except to criticize and punish. Also, he was away on business more than half the time." And the mother falls into a nervous overpreoccupation with the details of her own and the children's lives. Overprotective, even strangling, she still can't bear to hear any *real* criticism of life in the family because family is all she's got and all she is.

My own family fell into this pattern precisely. I knew my father loved me, but he was almost never home when I was a child. Working seven days a week, ten or twelve hours a day, he was an exhausted man when he finally got home, ate a late supper and took a look at his children. By then, my sister and I were asleep. If we were still awake, we begged him for bedtime stories. He told them to us, but we had to keep him awake so we could hear the endings. My mother, already struggling with her own depression, couldn't bear to hear that all was not well with us. We owed it to her mental health, I felt, to be okay always. There are limits, though, to how long you can keep up the perfection trip—all A's in school, medals at graduation. I kept mine up over thirty years. Not the world's record, but enough for the regional semifinals. Had I been able to mobilize my anger, as the young man in the last interview did, to run away to another city, I might have stirred up enough concern in the family to provoke a real look at my distress. I might have shown that I was a separate person who needed validation for my own style of doing things.

In the next interview, a father responds to his daughter's distress in the way I wish mine could have responded to me.

5. "I felt more like a person than a daughter."

A twenty-six-year-old woman, college graduate, an editorial assistant in a large publishing house:

My parents are both open and closed. They are interested in me and what I do, and they are pretty supportive (now—they haven't always been). Yet, I think they are often horrified at my "impropriety" (living in a communal house, not wearing a bra, and so forth) and mystified by some of my interests, religion, for example. I get the feeling that they gasp privately, but they don't get on my back openly anymore.

We are able to talk about lots of things, though sex and men are embarrassing for both of us, and we just steer clear of these topics. If I have a serious question or problem, I can ask my mother and she is very helpful. They are becoming politically more liberal, and we have pretty great discussions—heated, but fun. They are conservative about marriage, but don't care what I do for a living, just as long as it is something respectable.

I see them as pretty typically American Protestant middle class with the exception that they don't get overly involved in keeping up appearances. Yet, they are small-town people and like to be neighborly. Many of their values I find are important to me in ways I used to take for granted, until I got out in the world and found many people dishonest, irresponsible and unkind. Now I look at those beliefs of theirs and want them for myself. There are other things that I hope to be freer about than they, especially my mother. I don't think being reserved and ladylike necessarily means anything. I like to be lusty and even loud and sometimes sloppy. I also very strongly believe that it is vital for a woman to have a vocation of her own. No devotion to a man would be enough for me as it is for my mother.

My father is pretty interesting, and, as I get older and more involved in the world of practical things (after college and working awhile), we have more to talk about. He was rather a shadow most of the time I was at home, nice but very inaccessible. We did not really touch one another until a year and a half ago when I broke up with a man that I loved very much (he with me, rather). It was a bad time because I had asked for it in many ways. I had been heavily into the women's movement and was mouthing party line strongly. I had begun to discover how wonderful it was to have women friends, and I think I was afraid I would lose them if I wasn't radical. I lost Don instead, and that whole thing brought me up short to what I was really feeling. I was depressed, weeping all the time. I quit my job to travel and spent a few months at home instead. My parents were worried and incredibly supportive. For the first time in my life, my father talked to me about some of the things he liked about me (and things he didn't) very openly. It was a remarkable experience because in the end I felt more like a person than a daughter. He taught me about money (buying things on credit, getting loans, budgeting)—we talked about his work (he is an architect) and what it meant to him. I told him about my philosophical gropings and he listened until he understood. In fact, he sent me The Rebel *for Christmas last year. Ever since that time I have felt a genuine attention and acknowledgment from him which I am able to return.*

My mother during this time seemed busy and on the outskirts, which I later discovered was intentional. Amazing! She had encouraged my father to spend time with me because, "after all, he is a man." (Meaning, I think, that they, men that is, need to be understood.) She and I didn't become too much closer. She already knew a lot

*about me. But we did begin to get over the embarrassment
of talking about our bodies, emotions, vanity, and so forth.*

*In the past they tried to control me, and did, with guilt
and money. This business about being a lady was a big
problem for me for a long time. I am a little heavy and
never was able to dress in a way that worked, and I felt
socially clumsy for a long time. But looking back, I see
that clothes, looks and all that were a way my parents
used to subdue what they thought were dangerous impulses
on my part. I was kept feeling awkward so I wouldn't be
so "friendly to strangers." I was also vaguely ashamed
of my sexuality and am still dealing with those feelings.
These were all underhanded ways to keep me under
control, I think—also never giving me much money; what
I needed to survive and that was all. This was a way to
keep me from exploring the world by travel or doing
things that cost something. It forced me to start working
and earning my own bread so that they couldn't stop me
from exploring. They say now that they were afraid for
my safety, but I don't think they are really being honest
with their feelings.*

*Now they send a check once in a while for "mad
money," but we keep our finances very separate. The
episode with Don brought out in the open the fact that I
believe being a virgin when you marry is a barbaric cus-
tom. They were upset, but we finally agreed to disagree,
and I never bring it up. And I must say they don't make
any digs or remarks.*

*I have changed a lot in the past year, and I think that
period with my parents really helped me. We got to know
one another as people, so little things like buying gifts or
exchanging letters are far more personal and fun. I don't
think I would ever live with them again (unless it was an
emergency) because we would fight. If I conducted my life
the way I do, it would conflict too much with their style.
Also, there are internal parents which I am trying to get
rid of. They remind me too much of those images in my
inner "child self."*

*   *   *

In this family the daughter's despair was recognized, and the father moved in—not a patronizing, Daddy-knows-best style, but really *as an equal.* As a result of this encounter, "I felt more like a person than a daughter." They shared with each other the facts of their lives. The encounter strengthened her, made her feel validated as a *person* (not just Daddy's daughter). Notice that her father did not solve anything for her. The problem of grief after losing a lover, when you have mishandled the affair, usually has no *solution.* But getting support and validation for your feelings and your personal worth from a loved one helps you understand and overcome the pain, and you just get rolling again. When parents treat you like a separate adult person, you *become* more of an adult.

Mother missed a chance here, I feel. But it is genuinely in character for her, seeming to give way to the man in important matters. This is one quality, probably largely culturally determined, which her daughter is not going to emulate. Here is another instance that illustrates that even when values are very divergent between parents and child, parents can be vitally supportive in crises and come through for the child-adult. Perhaps one reason this daughter needed her liberation philosophy even more than some other women is the lack of affirmation by her mother that women are as strong and important as men. If the mother had solved the problem of how to love and be loved by a man without sacrificing her own equal status, she probably could have helped her daughter more during the struggle with Don, whom she eventually lost. But there are peers in the world from whom she can learn more about that.

6. "The most wonderful and intelligent child that ever walked the earth."

A twenty-seven-year-old man, a Ph.D. who designs computers:

My father died a year ago, but I never was able to really talk to him, not even just before he died. It still bothers me too much to talk about it. I have inherited all his tools, woodworking and photography. He loved gadgets, and I guess I do, too, but I am not going to let them come between me and those I love, as I feel they did for him.

I guess it is my mother we should talk about (though my sister is very important to me). When I think about it, there isn't too much I have to say to her. She can't understand my work (inventing with the computer) except by how much money I make at it. Women are an extremely difficult issue with me, and I certainly don't tell my mother anything about it, although my sister and I talk fairly openly. My mother (and father, too, I guess) did to me what I call the "only Jewish boy" syndrome. They told me I was the most wonderful and intelligent child that ever walked the earth, and that I had better take advantage of it or I would be wasting myself. They stuffed me with books, culture, a Ph.D., the whole thing. I have never had a satisfying relationship with a woman for longer than a month. I find it almost impossible to meet people casually and develop friendships in normal ways. It takes me a year of caution before I can trust myself not to be absurd. I have excellent "self-discipline" [sarcastic], and I am so frustrated and angry that I very often feel like punishing my mother—indeed in many ways I do.

She has always tended to cater to me, but it has been ridiculous since my father died. When she cringes and acts hurt, I can't help but pick on her. To keep away from that sort of thing, I keep away from her, see her as little as possible, write only when I have to. It's not that I hate her—I am just so angry. I have been told that when I work through all this I will be more objective about my mother and her characteristics. I don't know. She embodies a lot of what I don't like about women. She has done nothing with her life but wait on my father and fuck me up. She is a busybody. There is one incident which we still both remember, and which, in some ways, set down the limits between us. It was two years ago when I was home on vacation. I had been working very hard the past several months on my project and really learning and moving ahead. I was elated at how things were falling into place. I no sooner walked into the house than I was showered with cut your hair, change your clothes, you are a disgrace, and on and on. I reacted in my usual contrite way, though I was seething. I got a haircut, changed into my corduroys and tried to tell them what I had been doing. No response: I heard all about the neighbors, the business, the prices of this and that. I really felt very defeated and as though a film of pain dropped down behind my eyes. I hung around, going here and there with my father. Then one afternoon I came home and went into my room to change for dinner. My mother had taken my old blue jeans, my underwear, socks, some shirts and replaced them with all new clothes. I went berserk—I was both humiliated and outraged. Fortunately they were still in the trash. I collected everything, packed and left.

It might have been a little extreme of me, but I don't regret a minute of it. And I assure you, should anyone do that to me again, I will react the same.

I interact as little as possible with my mother, and go to my sister (she is ten years my senior, a doctor, married happily with three children) for help and acceptance. I am just now beginning to see (I have been in therapy for four months) that the impact of my mother and sister on me have really set the patterns for my relationships with women.

I have been thinking about the major changes in values between my parents and me. I can isolate one very very important factor: I want to be human among humans, not superman. I do want to be rich and make an impact on my profession, to fulfill myself as much as is possible, but not to be better than anyone else, as I think my parents saw me, but to be completely myself.

I reported this interview to show how praising one's child for his or her intelligence, potential, competence, and so forth can be carried to the point of controlling the child and making him or her become what the parent wants. Here, in the event of a confrontation, Mother could honestly cry out, "I was only trying to do what's best for *you*, dear!" The pattern of patronizing and infantilizing the son by fussing and criticizing is so obvious that it needs no more description. What is also clear, though, is how angry this makes children feel, especially during adolescence and young adulthood. Seen in contrast to the father's way of helping his daughter in the last interview, it is very striking. The relationship between this mother and her son is very likely to languish and die. He will turn to his sister, who probably treats him more like an equal, not, "Oh, what a wonderful son I own."

With the change from the extended family of much earlier times to the nuclear family of 2 parents and 2.6 children in America, a change brought on and encouraged by technological "advances," there are now only 2 adults in each family as resources for the adolescent in distress. Usually only Mom and Dad are there to recognize the symptoms of need for attention and guidance and to respond by offering what is needed in ways that will be accepted. This is why we now rely on guidance counselors and schoolteachers, shrinks and peers when vital contact is missing. But the fact that parents have known and nurtured the child from day one, been with him or her through sickness and pain, gives them such an advantage that the proper support and validation, if it came from a parent, would be far more effective than from anyone else. The validation must be for the young adult/child as a separate adult person, not a parent's puppet. When this happens, parents' guidance can be accepted and it will be helpful. When parents can't see and respect the boundaries of their child's separate self, their attempts to help will be rejected, met with rage—and they won't understand what went wrong.

7. "Nothing they could say could make me feel ashamed."

A twenty-five-year-old woman, divorced and a college graduate:

I don't know whether we communicate or not, my parents and me. We talk a lot of diddlyshit, but I make my decisions, suffer my miseries, live my life without much from or to my parents. I like them, I guess I even love them—they are simple and nice. I have several younger brothers and sisters, so I think a good deal of my parents' absence from my life is that they were just too busy to dote on me. This has had its impact on me, for sure, but I accept that as the reality for my life. I know they think I am okay (now at least).

Ever since we began talking about this interview about my parents, I have been thinking of my past with them. I asked Mother to talk with me several weeks ago about it. I think the real big break came when I was seventeen and got married and went to Canada. I had been a free baby-sitter at home for as long as I could remember, and sometime when I was fifteen or so I decided I wanted a few babies of my own (not as many as my parents had). I didn't want to take care of my brothers and sisters all my life or even a big part of it.

I believe my getting married got across to myself and my parents that I had desperately needed some time for myself without a great deal of responsibility, time to myself, attention just for myself. Of course, these insights didn't come until a couple of years later after Jack and I split up. I guess I am jumping all over the place here. I was in my last year of high school and feeling extremely pressured. I thought (and I think Jack encouraged this way of thinking because it was more true for him) that I was experiencing heavy sexual need and that it was probably a good idea to get married rather than be miserable and secretive about it all. (My parents weren't particularly religious, but they were old-fashioned about sex.) So we did. We kept it a secret until May. It was pretty hairy when we announced that we were married, and that as soon as we finished high school, we were going traveling and didn't know yet where we would settle down. The night I told my mother we were in the kitchen clearing dishes and feeling fairly hassled because of all the noise. I told her I had a lot of homework to do (end-of-the-year paper) but that I wanted to tell her something very, very important. I have to say that she stopped what she was doing to listen, even though it was way beyond what she expected (I think she would have been less shocked if I had said I was pregnant!). She called my father, and they both yelled and cried: what was I doing, I was so young, Jack had never worked (neither had I), what would we do if I got pregnant? Thinking back I realize what got me through all that was a deep well of anger which kept me from giving in to them. At the time I stubbornly stuck to my guns because they couldn't call me immoral or bad, stupid, maybe (which they did), but nothing they could say could make me feel ashamed. I even tried to express the pressure and unhappiness I had been feeling for so long, but they couldn't hear it—they being so pressured themselves. They eventually called Jack over and we hashed and hashed. I believe finally they were convinced that we were pretty decent and sincere and even though they were pessimistic, they agreed to recognize us.

We left a couple of months later and for the next two years we visited and wrote to one another, but I have always felt it was for form, that I was one of theirs, but not really a person. Even now when I am feeling more centered than ever in my life, feeling my personhood, I still don't think they can see me. I also don't believe it is malice, but rather a lack of education and worldly awareness; as I have said, they are too busy. I have suffered quite a bit because of having to find my own way: many wrong turns and no one older with whom I could talk. I

*developed a grumpy, self-protective attitude toward older
people in fact, because, as I now understand, I wanted
badly to be taken care of, loved—lasciviously loved. I
eventually got into school, and my father helped a little
(they were happy with that). Jack and I grew apart more
than anything else, and it was a relatively painless ending
for us; though how painless can it be when you say good-
bye to someone who helped you grow up? I am trying to
remember when I began to be dimly aware of my "psyche"
and its operations. I think it was in large measure the
budding self-consciousness of my friends and myself about
what our courses in psychology really meant. It was in
vogue to see a counselor, discuss Hermann Hesse, you remember all of that.*

*I have never tried to talk to my parents too deeply. I
have made it very, very clear that leaving home for me
was a need to establish my identity and they had better
expect various forms of that from the rest of their children.
I have never really been a child to them (only to myself),
so there hasn't been a big need to prove anything to them.*

Here's a good example of how adolescents who are not
in good communication with their parents can express a
need or a feeling through impulsive and shocking action.
"I believe my getting married got across to myself and my
parents that I had desperately needed some time for myself
without a great deal of responsibility, time for myself, attention just for myself." Was she afraid to ask her parents
for more personal attention and less responsibility? Would
they have heard her? It's likely that this girl needed more
of her own baby needs met, to be taken care of more, not
only to care for her younger brothers and sisters as a "free
baby-sitter." So getting married at seventeen looked to her
conscious mind like a way of getting out of being Cin-
derella at home, and unconsciously offered her someone
who (she thought) would give her exclusive, loving attention. Many of these early marriages act out needs like
this, but few can gratify them.

The account of how she told her parents she was married is very close to some of the scenes I have helped families through in family therapy. Through announcing her marriage, the daughter basically told her parents:

1. I'm through being your unpaid baby-sitter.
2. You haven't met my needs—I'm going off with someone who will!
3. I'm a separate person—I'll do what *I* want to do!

At a moment like this, parents are usually too devastated to get beyond their anger and despair. These parents finally accepted the situation, but what didn't happen here, and mostly does not happen, is an examination of *why* the daughter needed to get married in the first place. If Mother and Dad had asked her, "How have you been feeling lately about your life, and why do you think you want to get married?" they might have uncovered her resentment over the baby-sitting and the lack of attention, also her sexual neediness. Maybe someone could have suggested a period of time with free access to Jack, birth control, no enforced baby-sitting, and more concern from her parents. This might have had the good effects that the summer in Pennsylvania had for the young man in interview 4. In effect, a moratorium period, a set of new rules agreed upon by parents *and* adolescent, during which we see what will happen and we check in often to see how everyone involved is feeling. To encourage such trial solutions is one of my favorite techniques in adolescent psychiatry.

"I have suffered quite a bit because of having to find my own way: many wrong turns and *no one older with whom I could talk*." This is, unfortunately, not a rare statement from a young adult. Many families do not have the kind of closeness that permits a child to say, "I'm hurting." To take that chance, the child needs to feel confident that the parents can hear his or her own unique feelings and not simply react with suggestions as to how the child can behave in order to meet *their* needs. There are some techniques for parents to use in this situation—I'll bring them up later in the book.

8. "My father and I have shown our love to each other in quiet ways . . . it is enough."

A thirty-nine-year-old woman, married and with children, an artist who plans "to go to art school forever":

I think I understand the question, "How is your communication with your parents?" but it took a minute to remember when it all began to happen. It wasn't a normal course of events, that's for sure. My mother died of cancer when I was seventeen, and the couple of years before, while she was ill, I took care of her, my father and my two younger sisters. My father remarried about a year after she died, less than a year, actually, and we were absolutely appalled. We were young and terribly romantic. My sister and I were both in love with the men we later married, and we couldn't understand how on earth he could have done that. Of course, now we do; my mother and he did not get along so well because she was a spitfire and was always crossing him. She was very, very beautiful when she was young and a gifted musician. I suppose that is why he fell in love with her. Also, when someone you love is dying, love gets mixed up with loss and you begin to shut them out before they are gone, so it won't hurt so much.

At any rate, I was about seventeen when Mack asked me to marry him. Although we didn't get married till later, I was already committed and in a sense secure about my life at that time. I knew what he was going to be, that it was financially secure, what would be my role with him. Also, I was deeply in love. It's funny, but I remember that time and then look at all the transformations our relationship has undergone in seventeen years, and I realize that I love that funny man more now than I did then. He is important to this thing about my parents because he was my most primary source of support.

As I have grown older, I have tried to be more objective about what kind of person and mother my mother was. For years after she died, I romanticized her greatly—I think as a way to guide me as I became a mother. Even now, I am sure I can't be really correct about her because it was so long ago that she was alive. I remember her being sassy to my father, which he hated and we loved. I often had the feeling that it was "us girls" against him. My father was very tall, six feet three, with a gruff manner. He was a hunter and sportsman; in fact he fed us during the Depression on game and fish that he caught. During the week he was a banker, though we never had much money. Anyway, they scrapped a lot—something which I have never done with Mack in front of the kids (a reaction against my parents, I suppose). My mother, I remember, was warm and full of play. She would roll with us in the backyard and play hide-and-seek endlessly. Of course, when we were older, we would discuss boys instead. Up until geometry she helped with schoolwork. One thing about her was that she was very private. She didn't like our friends to drop in without making some kind of plans, so I always felt more comfortable playing at other friends' houses on a spontaneous basis. Now that I look back, I can see that it was my mother who was lenient and my father strict, but he had to be more so because she was so soft.

When she got sick, we had to be even more private about inviting people over—until we never did. We used to read to her and tell her stories. Oh, my God, she stayed cheerful. We, of course, didn't know she was going to die; I think she was the only one who truly knew or believed it. It was because of my mother that I ached and longed to be a singer. She was very musical, but to my never-ending sadness, didn't pass any of it on to me. I miss her terribly and wish to heaven that my own daughter could have known her.

My father is a different story. I was afraid of him most of my young life. He was the one who punished; he wouldn't let us wear trousers ever—pedal pushers were

*the fad then. "Young ladies always wear skirts . . ." He
kept a strict control over our young beaus, and, because
there were three of us, there were a lot of boys around.
I felt terribly sorry for him the last year my mother was
alive. He was withdrawn, and I once found him in tears
sitting in the car in the garage. He never talked to us
about his feelings, so even now he is a mystery to me.*

*The year he remarried was the year I graduated from
high school, and I left home to work and wait for Mack
(that is what was done in those days; it was wartime and a
sense of love and romantic loyalty pervaded our lives. I
would have gotten myself a career during those years, if
I had known what I know now). So, I saw my father only
a little. He didn't approve of Mack, and I didn't like my
stepmother. I guess the way I broke away from home was
just to leave and put my loyalties with the man I loved.
It was just assumed that we were grown—no one had time
for us to still be children. I don't regret it.*

*After I was married and had children of my own, I
began to get curious and also tenderhearted about my
father. I visited more often when I could, and eventually,
after about ten years of separation, we began to plan holidays together from time to time. He had gotten multiple
sclerosis, and each year I can see more deterioration. I
thank God he married who and when he did. She loves
him deeply and devotes herself to his care. If it weren't for
her, what would we do? He would live with one of us
surely, but that would be difficult with our young ones.
I respect her now as I never could as a youngster. She
has been good to us and for us.*

*I have never in my life had a serious or deep talk with
my father. I haven't even attempted it. I suppose I would
have if it hadn't been for Mack, but, over the years, my
father and I have shown our love to each other in quiet
ways and I don't want any more than that; it is enough.*

Very often a child who loses a parent in late adolescence
is fortunate enough to find a lover who can fill his or her
needs for love and support. This is successful when the

basic love needs have been met in early childhood. It can be a dead end if the adolescent is so deeply insecure and consequently low in self-esteem that a marriage "on the rebound" from losing a needed parent may simply add new problems. But this woman sounds as if she was pretty secure even in her teens and already well on her way toward a good love relationship. Moreover, it has lasted.

Another indication of her basic inner security and of her husband's solidity is that she has been content to come to know her father quietly and slowly, and to love him more over the years without traumatic confrontations or any specific deep discussions about each other's lives. I can understand this. It is how I came to know and love my own father when my mother's needs to control me and to dominate the family did not stand in the way. After her death, my father and I went through just such a quiet growth of love as she describes with her father.

Another point comes through. "After I was married and had children of my own, I began to get curious and also tenderhearted about my father." When we get into the parent role ourselves, we can empathize with our parents' struggles and failures, and we can recontact them, if they are still alive, with new compassion and understanding. I believe that there is a real drive within us throughout our adulthood to understand and empathize with our parents' natures, and in some way to face life as their companions. When parents can hang in during the adolescence and young adulthood of their children and handle the inevitable attacks and criticism *openly*, it sets the stage for later respect and love. The way parents deal with their adolescent and young adult children should reflect their confidence that time and the passage through the life cycle will surely help their children see and understand their parents' lives in perspective. If parents get shocked enough to close off communication or to break off emotional support because of some crisis of youth, that chance for later rapport may be forfeited.

9. "We cannot talk about anything real."

A thirty-year-old separated woman with children, who completed two years of college:

No, I cannot communicate with my parents at all. We talk now and then, but that is about all. My mother talks mostly about her illnesses and other people's deaths; her letters are all about who died or was killed, or who is sick. Here is one of her letters:

Dear Jane,

Hope these few lines find you ok. Its cool now and beginning to look like Fall; the leaves are turning. It seemed such a short summer with all the rain and smog. I hate to see winter come as that is the worst time for me. There seems to be something inside, a virus that just won't give up. Alice sent me up a big piece of garlic to put in my ear as my throat is sore. I got wet on the golf course Sunday and it didn't do me justice.

Doreen's father had a heart attack Sunday around five o'clock and is in the County Hospital. So far he's coming along good. Sarah was on her toes—he complained of indigestion and she said he broke out in a sweat. She called the Ambulance right away. Robert has a part time job at Jackson's—he called me and told me about Doreen's father this morning. Then I called Sarah—she was upset and said she took a tranquilizer.

We had a tragedy in the development. A neighbor, we knew him, was killed in an automobile accident— John Collins, 39 years old.

Doreen is working at the hospital so she can be with her dad. She will move in with her mother now— Sarah won't have to be alone. Glenda called me Sunday and said she had some tumors and they have

to watch her. *Don't know why they didn't remove
them when they operated.*

*Well, will close and hope I can have some cheer-
ful news some one of these days. I may go to Phila.
Tuesday with Dad. He has to go to turn in some
papers at the office. Will close for now. I'll never get
my teeth made. I can't get them to fit.*

> Take care
> Love,
> Mom

P.S. Dad is hanging in there with his blood pressure.

We cannot talk about anything real or important concerning my life. Certainly not sex; they disapproved of my
marriage though now they accept it. They are prejudiced,
conservative and closed.

My father is terribly defensive—he gets angry and ir-
rational if I even imply that he is doing wrong. I guess he
is that way in general. I can talk only very lightly about
politics, the cost of living, business (he is a salesman). He
is also an alcoholic, or, rather, on the road to becoming
one. He will pass out many nights—has bad blood pressure. He is also violent and threatening physically.

There have been two memorable events between my
parents and myself, though. When I was sixteen I wrote
myself a declaration of independence and have tried to
carry it through. I found it recently and reread it. Here it is:

My Declaration of Rights and Grievances

Attention PARENTS!

*Purpose: To create a better understanding between
my parents and me.*

*Grievance—There is no understanding or com-
municating among us.*

*General Rule—Most families are honestly inter-
ested in each other.*

Problem—My parents THINK *they are showing
enough interest in me when they ask me where I'm
going, what time I'll be back, and how much it will*

cost. Really, all they are doing is making me feel distrusted and afraid to ask for anything. A parent who is really interested in me, I feel, would get out into the open and show it by taking active interest in me by joining a few clubs in school for parents like other parents do, by going to the activities with me that I take part in, and by simply letting me share the things with them that are important to me as a teenager.

Problem—My parents do not understand that the things I do are very important and necessary to a girl my age. (Clubs, dates, school, etc.) They seem to think that because I'm only 16 I'm immature and don't know what I'm doing or saying. Because they're older, they think they know better what's best for me, but, if I, being "only 16," saw how badly this family is falling apart before anyone else did, who knows better? Right now I'm developing the habits and ideas that will stick with me the rest of my life. Through clubs I'm learning to help, cooperate and live with the people I'll be dealing with my life through—teenagers. Dating is very necessary and the most natural thing I could want to do because in a very few years I hope to have a husband of my own and I have to date boys of all kinds to learn to understand and live with them now so I can make my own home a happy one. School, therefore, comes first with me since it combines the other two things. You see, Dad and Mom, school isn't just a place for learning classic subjects, but it teaches social activities as well as studies. Ask any teacher, doctor or teenager and they'll tell you that dating and school activities as well as studies are making a future adult of me.

The money you're spending isn't being wasted. You both have the wrong attitude toward me. You think I'm just someone to help around the house and to spend your money. Really you should be glad that you can give me what you didn't have when you were my age. Housework, Mom, should mean to you a way *of teaching me to run a home, not seeing how much work you can shove off on me. You see, if this wasn't the impression you gave me, I'd gladly help. But, Mom, I remember when I was just a little girl and didn't want to do the dishes, you'd say, "What do you think I had you for?" I thought you were supposed to have a family to love and to give the things you yourself never had. Many times you've said, "If I had it to do over again I wouldn't have any kids." Does that mean—well, what does that mean? . . .*

I've got to learn to run my own life. Let me take getting home from a date for example: When a boy and a girl date now [1960] we have a set plan before the date. We usually leave around 7:30 and go to a movie. The movie, if a drive-in, lasts usually till 12:30 (the time I'm supposed to get home now) but, this includes, usually, two features. If you go to town it takes almost an hour to get there and one to get back. Either way, if we get hungry and want to eat we have to leave the movie early, so I can get home on time. This embarrasses both of us. Me, because not many girls after turning 16 have such an early time limit. Most of them have none at all, just so they don't come dragging in at 3 or 4 o'clock without a good moral reason, like a prom or a party. The boy is embarrassed because he thinks my parents feel they can't trust him or that I've done something I can't be trusted for. I have enough sense and self respect to come in at a decent hour. Besides, no boy respects a girl who has no control over herself. I do, but you haven't given me a chance to prove it. I got in at 2:30 a.m. once, but that was an accident. I knew myself it was too late to get in on my first date with a boy, but I didn't do it on purpose. Another thing. The neighbors should be your least worry. No one even raises an eyebrow at a teenager who gets home at 4 o'clock, let alone 2:30, here. Teenagers in every community set their own standards. People here don't think you're evil just because you get home late. They don't even think about it. I know, Dad. I know the local people better than you do because I deal more with them—I have more time and chance to hear what who says about what.

This was supposed to be an example of how I should be allowed to run my own life—because I'm ME. *I'm not like anyone else. I know myself best and how to handle my own affairs. I need guidance, examples and advice from both of you, but no set rules because of what you did or how things were when you were kids my age. These don't apply to me in 1960 either. Ideas, education, religion—the whole world has changed in all ways since you were my age. I alone know how to deal with situations that arise in my life because I must base solutions on how things are* now.

I hope I'm making you think and understand and not making you mad. I'm not putting all the blame on you, because I know your parents didn't understand you either. I know your home life was a mess, but that's no excuse for this home. Because of the War and other crises things were a mess when you were teenagers and when you got married. Homes were split up because kids HAD *to work to live. Kids quit school for the same reason. Can't you remember how it was? Now things are different. The world isn't at peace, but the U.S. is. Education and occupations are better and more secure and people have more time to live together. We don't! We never have parties for each other. I'm about the only 16 year old I know who hasn't had a party at* my *house so* my *friends can meet* my *family and see* my *home. I'm proud of what we have, of my father's job and my mother's beauty at the age of forty. I'd love to hear girls laugh at Dad's jokes and eat Mom's chicken. We never do special things together either, like picnics. Sure I always want a friend along! I need someone to talk to while the boys are fighting over who's the ugliest and Dad and Mom are complaining about some friend. I can't sit there with my teeth in my mouth all the time. I need someone to talk to.*

Can you see what I'm driving at? This family's got to learn to LOVE! *We don't hate each other, it's just that we've some awfully bad habits. . . .*

I wrote this because I love you all very much. Enough to try to help us. Please, won't both of you listen? I want you to tell me if I've said anything unfair. Writing can be misunderstood very easily. Then, I want us to talk it over and do something about it.

Please, let's try.

All my love to both,
Jane

I never gave this declaration to my parents, though I intended to. I thought better of it. If I had, it would have made things worse. Honest feelings, deep emotions like love always create chaos. I did send a similar plea after my wedding, which was a total disaster, between my own parents' nonefforts and my husband's mother's counter-efforts. Anyway, my father's reaction was that my letter showed I was "insane" to be unhappy about anything he or my mother had done and that my marriage must therefore be bad, and that he, Dad, had told me so. He had a good mind to drive up and slap me around a little, but he finally decided it wasn't really worth it.

For the next several years we just wrote superficial letters back and forth and saw them maybe once a year. My mother sometimes wondered about me. She despised having children and was, and is, so needy that she has very little to give and is never comforting.

The second and even more important event was about a year ago when I wrote a long, philosophical and real letter to my father telling him what I believed about life, and that I really loved him and Mother. This was some-time before Thanksgiving and I didn't get a letter back for the longest time. Finally, a week before we were supposed to go down, he called (I wasn't sure we ought to

*go, I feared he would be angry like before) and, among
other things, asked, "You think that love shit really works?"
I told him yes, I did. Later he said, "Please come home for
Thanksgiving." I still don't know if any one of the family
put him up to calling, though.*

*I believe under all this he knows I understand him and
under all his defenses he is glad that I do. I don't feel this
at all with my mother. She relates to me in a strictly
needy way.*

*I didn't communicate with either of my parents for a
long time and then began writing to my mother. She felt he
should not have written that letter, but she would never go
against him. Finally, for my son's first birthday, we invited
all the grandparents to celebrate. My father came and
treated us like clients. He can be very charming when he
wants to be. He slapped me on the ass, said I was looking
good and that we should forget the past. In fact, the only
way he is able to communicate good feelings toward me is
in some sexual way.*

*Now I don't have the desire to confront them anymore.
The change has come in me. There has never been a confrontation that has led to a positive change in their attitude
toward me. I have decided in essence that I don't have any
parents. I have given up the need to change them. I am
learning to relate to them without feeling sorry for them
and without creating any great disturbance. I am also seeking more from other people around me.*

*There was one person, my father's mother, who has been
the most positive and loving memory of my childhood. As
I said, my mother hated having children. When I was little,
I once swallowed some lye. I was very, very ill for a long
time, and my mother could not handle caring for me. So
my grandmother took care of me until I was about seven.
Those were truly happy times for me. She died when I was
twelve.*

This woman gave her father at least two chances to hear
her pleas. If she had given him her "Declaration of Rights,"
it would have made three chances. And there are clues that

he has some concern for her under his anger and need to be tyrannical. He seems comfortable only in the power position, especially with women.

One revealing item is the part about her grandmother, for whom this woman can thank God, because she was in many ways her real mother.

After her interview, my interviewer reported: "This woman found it very difficult and painful to talk about her parents for any length of time. . . . I find that most of the interviews have an element of this distress in them, indeed for me as well."

I have tried to help many authoritarian families by opening up communication between parents and adolescents, especially in my years as a military psychiatrist. It is a hard and thankless task. Advising fathers (or big-boss mothers) to let their adolescent children see their doubts, fears or feelings is often taken to be "foolish," and the rest of the family are soon forbidden to return for therapy. When you open up these channels, you turn the corner from postcognitive society, where the authorities need only say, "Do this because we say so," and you get to the much less secure territory on which a sixteen-year-old can tell her parents that she knows as much about life here and now as they do. Giving orders seems much more comfortable to many parents than negotiating with their own young.

10. "I am angry [with Mother] because she didn't solve her own problems."

A twenty-three-year-old woman with three years of college:

With my mother I can be as open as I choose to be. But, at the present time, I feel very, very angry with her and resentful. I am angry because of the kind of mother she was. This is all coming up in therapy now, and I am feeling a lot of old feelings that I can't separate from now. I am compassionately angry about her own life, which has been so terribly full of pain. She is in England now so we write, but when she is here we write, phone and visit.

Mother and I can talk about anything I want to—where I am at the moment, sex, men, religion, everything. The problem is that she takes everything I say and tries to apply it to her life. She looks to me for answers, though she rarely asks directly. She is a very moralistic person and smart, but she tries to intellectualize everything. She had a year of therapy and her way of attempting to absorb was to memorize what the therapist said. I try to help, but I refuse to answer the questions of her life because I know it doesn't make any sense. My examples may not be right for her.

I feel the pain I inflict on her when I withhold from her. When I was little, I used to join forces with her to protect her from my father (and brother, sometimes). Until now, I couldn't separate my anger against her from the fear that, if I were angry, I would be joining my father and brother against her. She has used many subtle, silent manipulations, making me and other people feel guilty if we don't give to her. She is a beautiful martyr. An example is the series of letters we wrote not too long ago. She wrote a long letter trying out the pros and cons of staying another year in England. I wrote back saying, "Perhaps I can help you out in deciding," but that I couldn't make the decision for her. She wrote a second letter saying that "Just because I have let you know the questions doesn't mean you have to answer them or help." She simply can't admit she is begging for advice from me.

She has been a very difficult kind of a mother. She was very prone to black depressions and, often, if she did things that she hated in herself, she would strongly react with guilt. She is very moralistic about right and wrong, and I am very angry that I have absorbed this. Her sexuality is conflicted as well (this is partly a responsibility of my father's as well—he never brought her out), and this has influenced me. When we were very young, she fell in love with my father's best friend and was going to marry him. But her German father browbeat her out of it, saying it

*was totally immoral and wrong, and that she should re-
member her children. So she stayed with my father. I am
very angry for her and for myself that she didn't leave him
then—or even later. She has done real damage to herself as
a result. It's never been good because she had a husband
who didn't appreciate her.*

*She can't accept praise and makes excuses when she is
complimented. She is very thin, and she never chooses to
wear clothes she knows are good-looking on her. I have
had the feeling that she is trying to live her life through
me. She tells me sometimes that I am more perceptive and
alive than she was at my age, or ever. Then, I get really
furious with her. I am angry because she didn't solve her
own problems. I had to feel her misery. Of course, I could
pick it up. There was so much sadness and pain in my
childhood.*

*I have been forced to imagine and to invent from my
twenty-three-year-old perspective what really happened.
There was so much pain I have deeply blocked. My mother
always said her mother was a saint, and that I looked like
her. I suppose my mother needed to believe it as an inspira-
tion or something.*

*My mother tries to force things to be whole. She simply
wouldn't accept that I was unhappy; she believed that if I
worked and did things that were active, everything would
be okay. My father always tried to joke unhappiness out of
me but I am who I am and that includes a lot of unhappiness. Now something very strange has happened. Fortunately, I am learning to see it. For me to let go of my
depression feels like a capitulation to my parents and a loss
of my sense of self. At least, my depression is* mine. *My
mother tried to manipulate me into being a musician: she
can't carry a tune. Also, I learned from her that men are
"bad"; and I am very, very angry about that, about all the
misconceptions of men I have gotten from her. Of course,
I can't blame her for feeling that way because that was her
life experience. Recently, I have been seeking a closeness
with men, trying to learn about them and to trust them.
Men are not trying to fuck me over, to use me or abuse*

*me. But I have absorbed some very moralistic and re-
ligious attitudes toward men. I am in a good and stable
relationship with someone now and, weirdly, I am angry—
I keep unconsciously trying to ruin it for myself. I do have
a fear that I won't be able to get the love that I need and
I worry about that. That's from home, I know.*

*My communication with my father also relates to anger
and therapy. When I was seventeen, my parents spent a
year apart, and I didn't really connect what was happening.
My senior year of high school was horrendous. I finally
stopped eating dinner with them because my father (a professor) would criticize my mother all the time for mis-
pronouncing a composer's name, or for overcooking the
vegetables or else they would want me to entertain them
so they wouldn't have to talk with one another at all.*

*When I was twenty-one I moved to New York and
shared an apartment with a former student of my father's.
Annette was her name, and, within a few days of my being
there, she told me that she had been my father's lover the
year before. We talked for about eleven hours straight, and
she told me everything. She was very compassionate and
told me in a way that I could handle. She told me how it
felt (emotionally) to sleep with my father—that he was a
little boy wanting to be a man. My mother actually knew
about this affair. When he began to get overwhelmed with
guilt, he broke it off and he and Annette couldn't even be
friends, at least at first.*

*That entire summer I was not on speaking terms with
my father. Then late in the summer Annette and I went by
his house and she stayed for dinner. Afterward he brought
her home—he'd been drinking heavily. He came into the
apartment and we sat on opposite sides of the room. He
started talking and saying he knew that I felt very badly
about him and his life, but that he loved me. Then he asked
me for some aspirin: "I need some aspirin, Sarah." It was
the first time he had asked me for something so directly,
and I was terrified. He kissed me good-bye (almost sexually) and said, "Sarah, you are looking beautiful these
days." It made me realize that from day one he had been*

asking me unconsciously to be his woman because my mother wouldn't. I was really frightened and threatened.

It was all very confusing. I felt almost that Annette was my mother and that, because I knew so much now, I had somehow almost slept with my father. I needed to feel Annette apart from my father, and, above all, a man of my own far away from father, too. After that summer I left for California to get away from all that confusion and everything having to do with my father. I needed to establish my own grounds and territory. I simply couldn't deal with all of it then; I needed to forget for a while.

When I came back here, I knew it was to deal with my father and my father inside me, and I now feel ready for it. I have been having regular therapy and making great efforts and progress.

When this woman talks about her mother, I get the feeling that there is a reversal of roles. Mother "takes everything I say and tries to apply it to *her* life. She looks to *me* for answers."

This is a common pattern in families. When a mother or father has not solved her (his) own problems of childhood and adolescence and has made an unsatisfying marriage, she (he) often turns to one or more of the children with the burning question, "What shall I do?" This can become terrifyingly direct: "Shall I divorce your father?" "Should I give up my unsatisfying career, but if I do, what will I do then?" My own mother used to confide in me her doubts about her marriage to my father. I remember the conflict this plunged me into: I felt selected as her confidant, involved in something central and very close to my mother. She had shared with me, at age nine, one of the central confidences of her life, but along with this very seductive closeness there came an awful sense of responsibility. How could I face my father now, having enjoyed the idea that I was closer to Mother than he was? This secret served to separate my father and me and to bind me closer to my mother in a seductive but extremely guilt-producing way. She had told me I was sensitive and intelligent like herself; she had honored me with bedroom confidences. Now I owed her more help and loyalty. In later years, I have come to feel that this was an unconscious power play—to enlist me with her and against my father in an undeclared marital war. Had they been honest, they would have left each other. These days they might have tried marital therapy. It would have helped or they would have separated.

Parents should never ask young children for heavy advice about serious life decisions. If they ask how the child feels about a change in family life-style or about moving or any *family* issue, it should be clear that it is a plebiscite, a referendum in which everyone in the family has his and her say, like ordering dinner in a restaurant: "What would *you* like, Junior?" And if there are price limits, the parents should establish them: "No, Alice, you can't order lobster. It costs nine-fifty," and so on. Parents should recognize which issues are personal and marital and make those agonizing decisions *themselves*. It is so much easier to spread the responsibility, in order to make a hard choice like divorce a little easier. "After all, the kids think I should get a divorce, too." But the guilt this produces is often unbearable. If what I have heard in my practice of child psychiatry is at all representative, many children have been trapped in this way into shouldering responsibilities that are not their own.

Only when children have grown up and appear to be making solid life decisions of their own can parents feel freer to share life decisions with these adult children. But even now discussions need clear labels. "*I* have been wondering . . . What is *your* opinion?" It should remain clear that the decisions are one's own, when all is said and done.

When she was twenty-one, the young woman in this interview learned of her father's affair. After the first shock, a lot of things began to make sense to her—her parents' angry distances from one another, her mother's long-term self-doubts and childish needs for advice and support from her children, her father's boy-man qualities. In a way the revelation has given her some vital realities to deal with, in the place of confusions. "What is wrong with my parents?" "Are all man-woman relationships like this?" Now she can see the neurotic roots of her self-destructive ways of relating to men, and she is trying to sort it all out in therapy.

I have come to feel that parents should be willing to level with their adult children when those children have become strong and independent enough to understand that they are separate from their parents and don't owe them any kind of behavior anymore. For example, when my twenty-one-year-old son was having some love problems, he came to talk to me. As I listened to the choices he was trying to make, whether to stay with someone he loved or to leave her because of the particular way she treated him, I suddenly realized that he was dealing with his lover in ways I had dealt with my own lovers in my early twenties. I saw that I could now offer him some advice that might save him some mistakes I had made and paid heavily for. But how to tell him that? I decided against putting it as "Dear Abby" counseling, but to keep it on the human-to-human level, revealing that I had had the same problems myself, made some mistakes in how I dealt with them and could only offer those experiences as material for him to think about. Whether he came to resolve the situation as I had or not was up to him. So I shared my own life experiences with him and told him why I felt that one or another choice I had made was successful or not, and stopped there. He felt he saw some new possibilities and went off feeling stronger. He later told me that he found the conversation useful and supportive, though he didn't necessarily feel he should or would solve his problem in any of the ways I had solved mine. The experience brought us closer together, and it has been repeated.

Parents could consider themselves and their lives as resource materials for their adult children. Like resource books in a library, we are there for our children to consult—we offer suggestions and styles of doing things, which they may or may not find useful. If they adopt our ways, well and good. If not, they will find others. Honest accounts of our failures are as valuable as our successes. If something our adult children do upsets us, we are entitled to say that we don't agree with them. But they will do what they will do.

11. "It can't ever be as bad again."

A twenty-nine-year-old woman, college graduate, working as a research assistant:

I can say that in many significant ways, important to me, my parents and I communicate; but, believe me, it hasn't come for free. I think a rather large chunk of my growing up has been directly related to them and their bossiness. We do not talk about sex, except to make jokes, but there aren't too many other topics that we haven't covered and with reasonable communication as well.

It began when I was a sophomore in college (I have always laughed at the term sophomoric . . .) and the guy I had been dating for over a year dropped me for someone else. I went into a depression that was quite severe, stopped going to classes, hid away in my room and just generally let my life fall down around my ears. I hadn't been all that happy before, but at least I had been hanging on after a fashion. But this time I was paralyzed. My parents drove up to see me (I hadn't written—the dorm mother called them), and, at first, they were angry at my self-indulgence over a boy. That pushed me even further into myself and all I could say was, "You're right, you're right, I'm weak, I am silly, you're right." I truly believed it. Shit, even now my blood boils when I think of that time. It's been ten years.

The upshot of it was that I withdrew from school and worked at a humiliating job as a waitress, living at home (terrible, terrible). I think my parents were trying to "knock some sense into me" about how rough the world was, and what I could expect if I didn't do well in school, and so on. We had a lot of visitors that summer, family friends passing through Washington and it was incredibly hot. One morning my mother got me out of bed at about 5:30 because she needed help in the kitchen. I was pretty damn sleepy. I had worked all day on my feet, and she stood in the kitchen bawling me out for not being helpful and for being so selfish. My father was away and couldn't I be just a little more thoughtful. This memory is still very vivid to me. Because I was so sleepy I must have been lifting my eyebrows to force my eyes open. She thought I was making a face roughly meaning, "What do you mean? I don't know what you are talking about!" or something like that. She slapped me across the face. I was so unbelievably angry that even now it is choking. I don't think I have ever felt so much hatred. I didn't say a word. I had no idea at that moment what kind of a face I was making. I can't remember what happened next exactly, but I ended up outside weeping and clawing my face (an unconscious reaction to my parents that I had done fairly often—can you imagine?). A neighbor saw me and ran to get me. I sat in her kitchen for what seemed like a long time. I couldn't tell her what happened, of course. What do you say? Finally, my mother came to get me. I don't know what kind of a mood she was in because I was so blindly raging that, when she came near me, I screamed and clenched my fists as though to pound her. "Don't you ever touch me again!" Much later I found out that that experience was as heavy for my mother as for me. It was obvious I hated her. It was quite humiliating for a neighbor to see all this going on.

I don't remember the specifics of the rest of the day, but I didn't go to work, I walked and cried, and by the end of the day, when my father came home, I was so guilty, angry, ashamed, confused and was ready to have the shit beat out of me. To this day I'll never know where my father got the presence of mind not to be angry—he wasn't at all. In fact, I felt his annoyance with my mother—a first, let me tell you. So instead of slitting my wrists (which I had been thinking of), I broke down. My father suggested I see a psychiatrist. That really frightened me because I wasn't at all sure I wasn't crazy and here they were suggesting I might be. That was the capper—I went to bed and didn't get up for several days. I didn't eat, slept, wouldn't talk and refused to see anyone. Finally, they suggested I go to stay with my aunt and uncle in Tennessee (I loved this uncle and his children were my age). I spent the rest of the summer there and toward the end I agreed to get some professional help. I felt a great deal of support from them— rode horses, messed around, was finally convinced I wasn't insane, just insanely unhappy. Being that unrelievedly unhappy can really get to someone after a while, and that was what happened.

Now that I have perspective on what was going on with me, I understand my desperation. I had no self-identity, no sense of who, what or why, in my life. Compounding this was the extreme difficulty I experienced making friends. I literally had no friends, no circle of stable acquaintances even, no means of feedback or support (the reason being that I was so unsure of myself). Neither of my parents paid much attention to me unless I did something wrong, so I felt very criticized most of the time. I think my mother was terribly insecure and consequently needed me to be less able than she so as not to feel so inadequate. She was also terribly afraid of losing my father (who kept her in that position). She fucked up my brother as well as me in many of the same ways, but my father and my brother had a good bond, so he didn't go downhill as much as I did.

I believe now that my parents do really care about me, else they would not have been willing to open themselves up to understanding what was wrong. Because of how bad things got, they made quite an effort, the result of which has been that their own relationship has improved and we as a family now have insight and language to talk about our real feelings, instead of being ashamed of our fears or angers, and to deal with all our personal feelings of wanting to accomplish something useful in the world in ways that don't turn them inward. The other truly wonderful outcome of all this is the feeling that it can't ever be as bad again, and that the troubles, the scrapes, foibles are all rather funny—we laugh at them and each other.

It is so common that parents' first reaction to a problem arising in the life of an adolescent or young adult child is anger. And when the child is feeling bad, as this young woman was over her rejection by her lover, it only intensifies the feelings of guilt and worthlessness. "You're right, . . . I'm weak, I am silly, you're right." Yet there *are* ways for parents to deal with their own feelings of anger when a life situation appears to have blocked the "progress" of their child toward "maturity." One way is for parents to turn toward each other and share with each other the way they are feeling about their child's situation: "It makes me *furious* to think that a love affair has made Janet so depressed that she can't stay in college!" and so on. Then, by the time they talk with their child, these feelings are vented and they may be able to be more understanding, if not downright supportive. In this case, it seems to me that Mother had not found a way to deal with her anger at her daughter, short of slapping her face in the kitchen. In fact, as the daughter reports, ". . . later I found out that that experience was as heavy for my mother as for me."

Then the crucial event: Father had somehow been able to get over his own anger with her, or he just didn't feel angry. So when he came onto the scene, he let his daughter see that he didn't agree with Mother's position—"a *first*, let me tell you." And here, too, a moratorium was the first step toward solution. An interlude in Tennessee (just as in the case I cited earlier, the runaway prep-school boy had gone to the summer place in Pennsylvania). In both instances a period of time without immediate responsibilities gives the person a chance to regroup his or her forces and get onto a new path.

So often there is a messy crisis in adolescence or young adulthood which forces a family to look at the feelings they have about each other. If the parental response to an adolescent's foul-up is *purely* anger and disappointment, the response is likely to be counteranger, and a war escalates. But anger needs expression—it can't be ignored. Choked with anger, we can't feel anything else. So if the parents can share it with one another first, they can then decide if they want to express anger toward their child at the time. Sometimes they will feel they should, and, if so, they ought to go ahead. If you are a parent in this situation, when you express your anger, try to label it clearly. Rather than, "You stupid, clumsy, oaf—you're always fouling up!" say, "This or that action of yours makes me very angry!" Show your grown child clearly *what* he or she did to make you so angry—that it is the act or decision that has you enraged, not the child. Expression of parental anger can lead to growth in teen-agers or young adults IF:

1. They can see what they did that made the parent angry.
2. They are not made to feel they are hopeless failures who always will mess things up.
3. They are given a chance to express their own feelings about the situation, including their own anger.

Expression of anger in a family must work both ways. If parents are going to express theirs, children must be free to express theirs, *and to be heard.*

Finally, there needs to be someone in a family who can say, "Okay, we've all let off steam—now what can we do to help?" And if parents hang in long enough to help the child make some positive life moves, the child *will* feel supported and more able to take positive steps.

12. "I don't know if we will ever really talk to one another."

A twenty-six-year-old man who finished three years of college:

My communication with my father is both very superficial and infrequent. We are generally able only to talk about how he is, what his immediate plans are, and what parts of Florida he has seen recently. For the last three years we have had almost no opportunity to talk. It is nearly impossible for him to communicate with me in any depth—he just seems incapable of it. Consequently, I can't really trust him at all. I was adopted by my parents, and I was the only child.

When I was eighteen and nineteen I tried to communicate with my parents when I would come home from college, being a little more insightful because I had been away. We never got very far; the old patterns were too strong for me to overcome. I was very rebellious when I was young, and when I would get impatient with my father and fight back, he would be both angry and frightened—and it would get very heavy until we would dissolve with guilt.

My mother is dead now. I had not talked with her for nine months before she died. It was around Christmastime and she called to find out what I wanted for a gift. I told her I needed a winter coat, a good heavy one. The one I had in mind cost $45. She replied that she only wanted to spend $30 on something I needed. I asked her why she couldn't, just for once, give me all of something I needed. She told me to get a job and earn some money. I hung up the phone. It was just like a thousand other times when I have asked for something and she would only be partially there. When I was ten or eleven, my mother's drinking problem became really bad. My parents never got along, and this made it even worse. I finally decided in my head that I had no mother. She would try to be affectionate only when she was drunk; otherwise she gave very little. I used to punch her to keep her away when she was like that. I developed a formula that on her drinking days I had no mother, that she was really not there; I began living in my head. My father would get violent when he got angry, and he would hit me (until I got bigger and could defend myself). I think my mother tried when she wasn't drinking. I can remember a few times when she would go to some home to dry out. My father and I would miss her and try to make things better when she got home. But it didn't work. After I left home, nothing much changed. I finally learned to depend on them less. I got a job and money of my own, got married, and didn't have to go back to their house. I have so many unresolved feelings.

When I was twenty-two, I came back from a trip with the woman I later married and found my mother walking out the door with all her things. When I asked where she was going, she just said she was leaving, that my father was awful and she couldn't take it anymore. She wouldn't tell me where she was going, she just said she was leaving and she was afraid I'd tell him where. If I hadn't come home on that day, I wouldn't have known. I was totally torn apart, devastated. It showed me how much I really needed them. My father tried to pull me over to his side by saying how terrible she was, always drinking, and now she had left us. Then he felt terribly guilty and remorseful: "What shall I do?" In the past when mother was drinking, he would ally himself to me, and try to get me on the band-wagon. It was painfully confusing for me. The other ways he would try to manipulate me were taking away material things, like the car, or telling me how much I had cost him that year, or how much he had put out for me. He also would say to me in a hundred different ways, "I'm suffer-ing!" but I never knew how to help.

Because my father was so weak, it is extremely impor-tant for me to have the male figures I do, like Don, the man I work for. Don and I are very involved with each other. He can put it to me; he also shows me what is important with his own life as an example. I had a fight with my girl last week because I felt I was doing all the pulling in our relationship, but I was missing the point. I have to learn to see more and Don pointed that out to me. He made me see that she was busting her ass to give to me in many ways, and I hadn't seen it.

I got back at my father in ways, too, a pattern I am still trying to break. When he would want me for something, ask, "Son, will you do this for me? I need help!" I was so tense—the whole situation was so horribly tense—that I would go to my room and sleep.

Now with my father I just try to let things go. He called

Christmas Eve because he had sold his business (where we had lived most of my life). He will be sixty-five in March. It was the last night he would spend there, and he was feeling low and I suppose nostalgic. When I began to reach out to him, saying it upset me a lot, he changed the subject. As soon as I began to offer, he swept it away. "Well, I'm getting a new trailer; I'm going to Florida." I don't know if we will ever really talk to one another.

In this very disturbed family there is a kind of communication in action. Everybody sees the other members as deprivers, frustraters. So the style is to wait until someone needs you, then withhold from them, saying, "You didn't come through for me when I needed you, now I won't come through for you." This provokes rage and retaliation. In such a family, a child could not learn the lesson of how to give. But if you are already angry and deprived, you are in no mood to reward those whom you know have deprived you. How could this young man, already feeling himself to be a victim of his mother's alcoholic inconsistencies and of his father's needy rages, find in himself the maturity to overlook his mother's way of giving him a present? In a family where love had been more available, Mother might have said, "Look, son, I have only thirty dollars, but I want it to go toward something you choose." And the son could accept this as a genuine gift of love, but with financial limits. She'd have felt good as the giver, he'd have felt good as the receiver. But here the years of no one getting what he or she needed have soured everyone. They all know how to deprive and be deprived, not how to give and receive love. Far too many families work this way. We can see how this man must now overcome the influence of such programming. He finds it hard to see how his girl gives him love. He can identify the merest whiff of deprivation, but can't recognize love and giving. He's simply not used to them. Now in young adulthood, he turns to other parent figures like the man he works for, and begins to see that there are other ways. He has learned enough and grown enough so that he is able to offer to share his father's sadness at the end of his business life in the town they had lived in for so long. But even this attempt to share feelings is rejected.

13. "I can't believe [love] is all that mush."

A thirty-three-year-old grocery store owner, a college graduate in economics:

My father committed suicide when I was fourteen and my mother died of a heart attack a year and a half later. I have never forgotten one moment of those two events. I was then taken care of, such as it was, by my aunt and uncle (Mother's brother; they were quite close), and it is to their home that I go on holidays. My father killed himself because (so it seemed) of a big failure in business. I have never understood. I believed there must have been much more to it all than I was told, or perhaps more than people knew. I have always felt that if he loved me, he wouldn't have done that. Even now, when I have a son of my own, I feel the same.

It is hard to remember in detail what it was like with them. My father was away a lot when I was young, and I was with my grandparents, my mother sometimes, and servants. I remember being happy, doing all kinds of things, playing, riding, sailing. I went to school, of course, but I was never very good at school and got through it as quickly as I could. My father would tease me in a way that I could see through; he didn't know how to talk personally (with me anyway), but he would explain things to me at the time. If I asked how something worked, he would very patiently tell me. When he was there, I remember him as very nice and somewhat awkward. He was very handsome and I remember feeling proud of him. It really is difficult to remember him because he wasn't there much. I have incredible sadness about him, and until a few years ago I used to build images of what he would have been like if he were alive. (I figured out that they were dreams of what I wanted for myself—no reality to them.)

My mother I remember somewhat more clearly because we did more together. She was very purposeful, and when she wanted something, she talked about it endlessly, figuring out how to get close to this person, cultivate that person, learn how to fix a certain food. She was very serious about her "social duties," and it was because of her that we got involved with the people that we did. She studied things and learned how they were done. She was the one who disciplined me, but rarely was it firsthand. I used to fight a lot and I was quite disobedient, not for any reason, but because I hated to be told what to do. She would hear about this from someone else and before dinner we would talk. She would say that she had heard something or another—oh, that I had pinned Charlie with my knee on his windpipe and scared him, and she would say I had to stay in that night and the next, or that I would miss doing something like a horse show or something.

Many times the three of us would take a trip together. There are many summers I remember. They seem so light and easy, I don't really have any words to describe them. My parents always seemed calm with each other; though now that I am older, I can't believe they were really like that.

When they died, I stayed with my aunt and uncle for about half a year. It was really, really bad. I was in trouble a lot (the same things always), and once when I came home late, my aunt must have been worried. Anyways, she met me at the door and said, "No wonder your mother died, you are so difficult to watch." I was upset by that quite a bit and left their house, ran away, soon after.

They sent me to prep school in Maine for the next three years and I was very happy there. Life was quiet and beautiful. I had a friend who was with me all the time, and I felt good. I went to college, got married at twenty (we had to) and went to work on Wall Street. Things went too well and I began to fuck up. I am told

I need a constant challenge; somehow everything there was too easy. I was divorced after four years of marriage, married again, divorced again. I don't know, I like things to be easy and straightforward. I moved to Vermont for that reason and I think I will stay. I like the people and the mountains.

I think it was my parents' absence more than their presence that has shaped me. I find it profoundly difficult to expose myself, and I don't like to get too involved with anyone. It feels like a jungle. I like people, but I think I am really quite a loner. I am also not sure I have loved anyone. I don't even know if I am able; I'm not sure. Does anyone know what love is? I can't believe it is all that mush, I simply cannot believe it.

In this story of suicide and loss, this man says something I have heard many times in therapy: ". . . if he [my father] loved me, he wouldn't have done that [killed himself]." Children very often absorb the guilt for a parent's suicide, and frequently this disastrous blow to their self-esteem makes them feel deeply unlovable and in the end keeps them from finding love and closeness. If such disasters can happen unexpectedly, and if they make you feel that you have failed to be lovable enough, it's much safer from here on to avoid closeness and its risks. Certainly this man has lifelong reservations about love. He cannot trust human involvement. For this reason he has sought an environment where he can keep a greater distance from people. But I wonder how he can teach his son what he himself cannot experience.

This brings up a larger issue. Just as young people feel devastated in their self-esteem when a parent commits suicide—"If I had been a better child, he or she wouldn't have had to do that!"—adolescents very often find that, when their parents are deeply unhappy, they themselves cannot feel the right to find happiness. It feels just too selfish to grasp life and make it give you what you want when your mother and father are so obviously miserable. As in the case before this one, parents need not only to show children in the early years what love is, but also in adolescence they need to help children see how one goes about grasping love and satisfaction from the world. If parents fail to do it, their children find it too guilt-provoking to do it for themselves. There is a tendency then to settle into a life-style with less risks and avoid trying to reach for what you don't think exists or what you wouldn't feel any right to enjoy. Such a style may be safer for someone with the life history of this man. But when his son becomes a teen-ager, I'd suggest that he share some of these feelings and the life experiences from which they grew with his son. If he says, "Son, my parents died when I was young, and I was plunged from happiness into despair; I chose not to be a lover—involvement feels too much like a jungle to me. I find it profoundly difficult to expose myself," his son may be able to see how his father's life-style results from his father's earlier life, but that he need not follow his father's decisions.

Knowing how parents became what they are liberates adolescents to be themselves. They can separate themselves more easily from the deeply felt obligations to live up to the needs of their parents. Later in the book I will go further into this issue of how parents can tell children who they are, and thus liberate the children to be who *they* are.

Earlier, notably in the cases of Henry and Peter, I went into the issue of how hard it is to clear up the emotional blocks and internal images of parents left inside you when parents can't accept the reality of how they behaved during your childhood. Henry and Peter must do most of the work of developing self-esteem without the clarifying experience of honest encounter with parents: "I did this because . . ." "When you did that, I felt . . ." and so on.

The man in this interview has the same problem because his parents are no longer alive. But he can deal with the image he carries inside him through therapy. In a relationship with a therapist, he can come to see what his real needs are and how he really feels. He could reach a point where he feels safe to take the emotional risk of attempting a relationship—therapy could teach him how to reach for love.

14. "[My parents] are no longer my guides, except as individuals."

A twenty-four-year-old carpenter:

My parents and I can talk about many things, but we disagree on almost all of them. I don't feel they receive me emotionally. They think I am weird.

We have talked about most things that concern my life—sex, money, life-style, all that, but I have never felt they approved of what I did. Sometimes they actively disapproved.

My father has very different work values from mine. He grew up very poor and always wanted to protect himself from terrible want. He has always wanted to better himself, so whenever I want to do something that isn't financially secure, he worries and complains. I do not look to money for security. I guess I have always had enough. But I feel security or insecurity about the people I know, and wonder how well I know them! Sometimes I really do worry about being deprived of the company of people.

My father doesn't worry that I will be a menace to society any longer. I believe they accept that I am a good person, but it wasn't easy. I didn't finish college, and then I went to live with Doris, and my parents were in an uproar. They really condemned me as an evil and immoral person. I didn't communicate with them, and even told them once I hated them. They were really upset then, and all my mother could do was cry. My father kept saying, "Oh, my God, oh, my God." Finally, I left their house and didn't come back for months. Sometimes my mother would call but I would barely talk to her. Once she hung up when Doris answered the phone, and I don't think she ever called again.

When Doris and I broke up, I was down for quite a long time. At that time I began to realize how important

*my parents were to me, and that I really needed them. I
went back to visit—I think I wrote a letter first. Anyway,
I went back for supper one night, and it was just the three
of us. It was really awkward at first because they didn't
know what I had been doing, and I don't know if they
still loved me. My mother and I were in the kitchen not
saying too much, and I became overwhelmed. I just hugged
and hugged her, telling her that the kitchen smelled so
good. She cried and my father came in and we talked about
things. I forgot what all we said, but mostly it was just
that we loved each other and that the time apart showed
us just how much.*

*It has been both nice and difficult since then. I think
they are finally beginning to realize that they are no longer
my guides, except as individuals; not as parents, I mean.*

*My parents can force things out of their minds if they
are troubled by them, so lots of times it is hard to know
what they are thinking. They don't know themselves. I
rarely relate to them on more than a superficial level.
With my father I talk about carpentry, and when some
people moved into my house, he wanted to know all about
them. But what my parents really wanted to know was
what they did, how much money they made and did they
have boy- or girlfriends—in other words "the facts." Still,
I think they are happy I am not living alone anymore; they
did think living by myself was bad for me. My father
especially is a social person and loves to talk—indeed, he
doesn't like silence.*

*I am closer to my mother. I am quite fond of her. She
has grace. We don't talk about anything deep, however.
I sometimes help her make a meal and we don't talk at
all. I guess what it amounts to is that their life is already
formed and they can't accept anything too extreme or
different.*

*As far as better communication is concerned, there are
a few things that have changed. Most of all it is me. I
stick to what I believe because I really believe it, and I
won't let them push me or talk me out of anything, though
they do try to make me feel guilty sometimes when they*

don't care for something I'm thinking or doing. As long as I am explicit about my feelings and strong, they will let me be, even when (and it is often) they disagree. I think they have changed insofar as now they only want me to be happy. How I do it doesn't concern them much anymore. Also, I see them as people, both interesting and vulnerable and sometimes wrong. I make my own decisions. Because they live so close, it sometimes takes work to keep them from interfering in my life.

It's funny to talk about them this way. I think I realized while you asked questions that my parents are really a major portion of my consciousness. Whether in fighting them off, shaking out their criticisms or finding ways I can relate to them, it takes a lot of time.

This situation is interesting because it starts with a big family battle and the breakoff of communications between parents and son. But unlike some of the other families I reported on, communication was reestablished. It is interesting to see how this was accomplished.

To begin with, these parents put themselves in a very polarized position when they condemned their son as "evil and immoral" over going to live with a woman. Had they advised strongly against the move, given all their reasons, but acknowledged that at twenty he had a right to run his own life, there could have been an ongoing dialogue. Even if his mother had dared to take a less extreme position than his father, as I suspect she wanted to do, she could have kept in better touch, and this young man would not have felt that he had to stay angry and defensive for so long.

As it was, there had to be a breakup with his lover for him to see that he still needed his parents and to dare to go back to them. At the moment of their reunion, it is vitally important that the parents as well as the son were able to acknowledge that they all loved and missed each other, despite their earlier judgments against what he had done. Had they insisted that he confess wrongdoing at this point, all would have been lost.

Obviously, in this family parents and son don't agree on most important issues. The son has found ways of dealing with this. Mostly he keeps things superficial, but he has learned from the fight over his affair that *"as long as I am explicit about my feelings and strong, they will let me be, even when . . . they disagree."* This is an insight many of the young people in this book have arrived at, each in his or her own way.

". . . my parents are really a major portion of my consciousness. Whether in fighting them off, shaking out their criticisms or finding ways I can relate to them, it takes a lot of time." Parents are a major portion of any adolescent's consciousness, and their judgments of his or her behavior can be devastating. Even after their children grow up, parents retain a direct hot line into their self-esteem and feeling of basic goodness or badness. They were the original trainers and they can make their grown child feel guilty when no one else can. This puts an adolescent or young adult into a terrible bind when he or she feels a deep need to take an action the parents object to. If he or she goes ahead, he or she will have to override the deep parental voice inside which comes up from childhood, saying, "They're probably right and you are doing wrong!" Combined with strong parent voices, using terms like "evil" and "immoral," this inner parental voice (the old superego) has forced many an adolescent or young adult to break off a love affair, stay in college, keep a hated job, and so on. In terms of daily life strategies, the parents' advice may be wise. But my point here is to show the reader that the cards are stacked heavily in favor of parents' opinions. The adolescent or young adult has a lot to lose, not only in terms of his or her parents' material and emotional support, but internal feelings of guilt and "badness" if he or she defies them.

However, there is a heavy price to pay for going along with the internal and external voices of the parents, though. When I was fifteen I fell in love with a girl at high school. We were inseparable for a year. When my mother found out we were so close, she stepped in and put pressure on me to break it off. "You're both too young to be so serious. You have your career to think of. This is too intense for fifteen-year-olds." Many a teen-ager has heard these words, God knows. I couldn't stand up to her. I broke off the relationship and felt ashamed I had done so. For years I felt angry with my mother and ashamed and weak within myself. I had to rerun the whole conflict a few years later when she objected to my getting married. By now I was stronger, and I acted more like the young man in this example. I went to live with my girl and went on to marry her, though my mother swore she could not live through it.

Even at twenty-one, when I married, I could not have put into words what this young man expressed—basically, that the struggles against parents' judgments during adolescence do teach some vital lessons:

1. Parents are a large part of your consciousness and defying them is costly. You miss them and need them if you're out of touch.
2. You *can* do what you want to do even if your parents object, but you had better be sure inside yourself that you are right and be very clear with your parents as to what you're doing and why. As this young man put it, "As long as I am explicit . . . and strong, they will let me be, even when . . . they disagree."
3. Parents can be wrong and often are.
4. *You* can be wrong just as often.
5. Open communications between yourself and your parents feel better than when they are closed. People who love each other deeply can and do disagree deeply, but disagreement does not mean the end of love.
6. Battles in adolescence with parents are inevitable, and if you keep communications open during and after the battles, you will have found out a lot about

who you are and who they are. This is information
you must have to develop a genuine identity that
is really you.

15. "Though they always want to know, they don't really want to hear."

A twenty-five-year-old photographer, a college
graduate:

My parents and I can communicate, but not really.
Whenever we begin talking about things that they have
strong feelings about, they get very dogmatic. For ex-
ample: sleeping with a woman before marriage is decreed
bad; making a living as an artist is bad; drugs are bad; the
black problem immediately becomes the nigger who owes
my father $400. When I tell them about my plans or
activities, they are threatened, mystified and sometimes
angry; though they always want to know, they don't really
want to hear.

They have never liked the girls I have brought home;
they don't like my friends, so I don't bring anyone home
anymore. About my studio: the first time they saw it before
I had a chance to fix it up, my father told me to move out
immediately and he would pay the rent anywhere but
there. The next time, when I had it fixed and more like a
home, he loved it. In other words, they will (most of the
time, not always) support something of mine when they
can see it is falling together. They do not trust my ability
to put something together from raw materials that I have.

They try many kinds of control, but this usually doesn't
work anymore. They refuse to support my music or art.
They offer plenty of money for medical or law school. In
other words, they practice selective economic boycott.
That is just about the only way I let them intrude on my
life anymore. But this has only come after a lot of pain
on my part. One of the most significant memories about
this manipulation was when I was a sophomore in college
and was accepted for a study-travel program around the

*world. My father refused to support my trip and I backed
down. I almost killed myself, I felt so inadequate and
upset over it. Now, looking back, I think my father was
jealous, that he has never grown up himself and couldn't
accept my growing independence when it was crucial for
me to have it.*

*My experience of my parents, my father especially, is
that he is critical. If I got 95s on a report card, they
should be 99s. So, when I got Cs in college, he assumed I
was goofing off, never a thought that perhaps I was
troubled. They would try to get me to do what they wanted
in very underhanded ways. My father always griped about
how much money it cost for me to go to school. He would
show me the accounts of how much I "cost." They would
never attack openly or be honest with their feelings. They
would launch rockets while I was sleeping.*

*The way I dealt with it was by not coming home from
school, or when I did, I would disappear into my room and
not talk. The other thing I did was ask them to pay for
therapy, which they finally did.*

*They are very set in their beliefs, very unmitigating
about their way. They believe their environment should
adapt to them! For example, we had a cottage on the
beach, and when the state took it over for a public beach,
they said forget it and never got another, as though they
had been defeated. They were sure my sister was a virgin
when she got married (because they wanted her to be),
even though she and her boyfriend would go away for
weekends together. By the same token, they think my
brother is bad because he is more open about his relationships with women.*

*They are politically very conservative (Nixon is hon-
est!) and believe in individualism, professionalism, serving
people but making money (a must). Yea, Horatio Alger!*

*I believe in the physical side of life. I like exercise, both
of body and thought. I want balance in diet, spirit, beliefs.
I believe in freedom rather than just thinking about it.
And in obedience to discipline and healthy ways. I want*

to make a living doing what *I* want to do and being in charge. *I* don't want to get legally married, but *I* really do want a family.

I am not as afraid of things as my parents are. *I* do not need to create prejudice or stock responses to protect myself; *I* feel *I* can confront life and deal with it. *I* was brought up in a rigid family system, went to a Catholic high school. College was very cosmopolitan, and the shift was so drastic that it was desolation row, emotionally the hardest period of my life. Now *I* have built security on a different structure from them. They simply can't recognize it.

The next and most important event with them was when they told me *I* was adopted. It was Thanksgiving last year, and when *I* got home, my father got all dressed up and said, "John, Jr., we are going for a ride." (He had done this for the last two holidays, but we had just ridden around and talked and come home.) This time *I* pulled over to the side of the road and forced him to tell me. In fact, *I* said only half seriously, "Are you going to say *I* was adopted?" He said, "Yes, you are." We fell into each other's arms and cried. He was afraid that *I* would reject them once *I* knew, and they would never see me again.

For me it was especially important because *I* realized *I* was both biologically and socially separate from them. We have been able to establish more mutual respect. There was a time when *I* rejected almost everything about them. *I* never wanted to eat tomato sauce again. *I* felt there was nothing happening at home but TV. They felt that living was a chore.

It was about a year ago that *I* began to confront them as people. *I* don't ask for support for what *I* do and *I* like my mother's cooking now. (*I* have met many people in Boston whose reality is so different from my parents'— people who are inspiring me, for whom living is a joy, who can love without so many of the sticky aspects.) By not asking for much, the conflicts between us are minimized. *I* can be less critical and can laugh instead of yell or with-

draw. If they try to do something to me, I just say no. If they yell, I do; if they slap, I do. Now our relationship is more equitable. What they say is not so important to me; I can trust myself so much more.

The incident of the study trip recalls the comments I made on the previous example about giving in to external and internal parental pressure. Notice how this man felt upset and inadequate over backing down, just as I did over a girl at fifteen. But later he sees the reasons behind his father's objections: "My father was jealous [of me] . . . he has never grown up himself and couldn't accept my growing independence."

Parents are so often jealous of the opportunities they have made available for their young adult children, opportunities they themselves did not enjoy: the chance to go to college and graduate school, to take extensive and expensive trips, enough money not to have to have a job all the time, the chance to select a career by choice, not financial need. Parents should recognize this jealousy and many do. It is not so weird to be jealous of your children if they are getting what you did not. And an important part of communicating with them is to recognize and acknowledge the jealousy rather than act it out, by selective "economic boycott," for instance, as this young man calls it. If you don't want to support some plan your child thinks up, then don't support it and tell him why. If you are jealous, admit it; it only means you are human. Many parents, unable to admit their jealousy of their children's opportunities, think up other plausible reasons for objecting to their projects—"You're too young, not ready, you'll get in trouble." But such reasons are usually detected for what they are. The child feels you are deceiving him and finds ways of retaliating.

It's hard to keep vital facts from children. In this adoption incident, the son already half knew the truth. So when his father told him, the key event was a *feeling* exchange between them; they could cry together. This brings up an observation I have made over and over again: when the feelings between parents and children are open and honest, there can be huge disagreements and differences in values, but the family is healthy.

Many parents in middle age find themselves subtly frustrated and depressed. Having enacted "The American Dream," having fought our way into a position that our own parents would respect, we find that peace of mind still eludes us. Surrounded by expensive possessions, high in the economic and status ranks, many of us still feel an emptiness; *something* has passed us by. Looking at this enviable freedom of movement and choice of young people and their avoidance of commitments, many of us either condemn them as "irresponsible" to cover up our own frustration with our own lives, or (more and more of us) shed our responsibilities and try to live our twenties over again at fifty. The number of divorces after twenty- and thirty-year marriages is growing, and more and more middle-aged people are giving up boring jobs and changing direction in midlife. Sometimes this works, sometimes not. As one lawyer said after he uprooted himself from an asphalt jungle and moved to Hawaii at fifty, "I moved heaven and earth to escape the rat race, and I found the mouse race!" We must face our jealousy of our adolescent and young adult children. They have longer to live than we do, and they are avoiding some of the traps of commitment and overcommitment that we fell into. Many of them will cheerfully squander the thousands given them by grandparents and parents on impulsive travel and pleasure experiences. Though we see clearly that this won't make them happy in the long run, maybe we also sense that they are *at this moment* freer and more comfortable internally than we are. It's the age-old story of the wealthy town merchant envying the gypsy. And many middle-aged parents have found ways to combine some of this freedom, this here-and-now orientation with our responsible work-ethic lives. A friend of mine met a white-haired, seventy-year-old granny leaning on her cane in a tiny Cape Cod village. After exchanging a few pleasantries, the granny asked, "Would you like to come home and smoke a joint with me? I've got some lovely grass!"

If we envy our grown children their freedom of choice and movement, we should be honest about it. Why not let them know that we have mixed feelings about our responsibilities and achievements? We are *people,* not just identification figures for them. One of the young men we interviewed saw this clearly—"My parents are no longer my guides, except as *individuals.*" I advocate parents sharing their doubts about their lives with their young adult children. Someday they may be exactly in this position, middle-aged, having invested a lot in life and wondering what to do about it. Why not let them see how their parents are struggling with this issue? They'll respect the honesty and it will help them cope with hard choices, having seen their parents do it. We can still learn from *each other.*

PART FOUR

Accepting separateness

CHAPTER 9

Interviews with parents

I have included the following interviews in order to show the parents' side, their feelings as the adult-to-adult relationship takes shape.

1. **"[My children's] selves were more theirs than my responsibility."**

    This mother of three, an intelligent and creative writer, preferred to write down some of her memories and feelings:

    When John and I were married in 1947 he was a returned, decorated RAF pilot back at his five-pound-a-week job in the British Home Office. He had graduated from grammar school some eight years before and, without any financial means of going to university, had taken the Civil Service job. To him and to his Depression-scarred parents (who kept a bakery in a working-class part of an English town), this represented the best available security. In May of 1947, when we became engaged, John heard that university grants were being made to those veterans whose education had been interrupted by the war. He didn't qualify, but he applied. And he was accepted.

    When we set up housekeeping in London in 1947, John

began attending a college of the University of London devoted to science. He received a grant of five pounds a week from the government; the rent of the bombed-out flat we found was exactly five pounds. So we had a classmate as a lodger. The three of us spent the evenings huddled around a plate-sized coal fire (all the ration allowed), and while they studied, I listened to the BBC through the headphones from John's pilot helmet. John's concentration was supplied by tremendous pressures: He had not studied for eight years; he was breaking all family tradition by going to university; he was not building up his pension in the Civil Service, etc. He did nothing but work.

Two years later when financial things were easier because of my work for Time-Life International, I wanted a child. I was thirty and felt it was time. For John, it was another pressure, and he would not know for two years if he could qualify for the degree (English universities only examine students at the end of the four years on the entire four years' work). He acquiesced, but felt an added pressure.

Kevin was born under the National Health Insurance Plan. This meant that I attended a clinic at St. Mary's Hospital where the "antenatal" clinic was manned by medical students, and never the same ones twice. Pregnancy was easy for me, but it required persuasion to obtain a bed in the hospital for the birth. I was granted one because I had no mother in England to help me.

Childbirth was a big guilt trip for John. His mother, in keeping with her social and economic situation, never consulted a doctor until two days after his birth commenced. The result was that she could never have another baby and suffered for years from "the complications." Furthermore, she told this story at tea parties in John's presence very often. The result was that John would come to see me in the hospital after the birth of each baby and sit down by the bed and fall asleep.

He wanted children, and he wanted more than one to

avoid the "only-child" pressures he had felt, but he disliked the marketing arrangements.

Some weeks after Kevin was due to be born, I asked in the clinic why it was taking so long. This query made me the subject of the class conducted weekly by the chief of gynecology at St. Mary's, in a frock coat, and the class chiefly in turbans. Kevin's position was atypical, his spine lying along my spine, and the teacher tried to turn him, but he wouldn't turn, and after some projections about mortality in cases like this, which I remember as frightening, he told me to come back in a week to have the baby induced.

All of this made me pretty nervous. There was literally no one to discuss it with. When I went back, they gave me hot castor oil in a teacup and put me in a bed in a ward with thirty other mothers, all of whom had serious medical problems in birth or they wouldn't be admitted to hospital, or had lost six babies in the blitz or some similar tragedy. In this group I was The American; the implication was that I was less brave than the English. I felt they were probably right, but I was damned if I would show it.

After twenty-four hours in the ward, I was finally admitted to the delivery room but nothing happened, and the nurse-midwives decided to call a doctor. Ultimately they gave me gas and delivered Kevin with two pairs of forceps. He had cuts down both cheeks and bumps on each side of his head. They showed him to me and then removed him for a week, saying he was suffering from shock. We were in the hospital for three weeks.

I did not feel I had done a very good job and Kevin seemed to me a double miracle: as any baby is a miracle and also because of his apparent good health. Once he came home, he began to thrive, and if I still had fears about cerebral palsy, mental impairment etc., I was not aware of them.

John studied for the first two years of Kevin's life, obtained his degree and decided to emigrate to America. We came here when Kevin was eighteen months old with five dollars and a baby and, for John, the added pressure of having left a dying father in search of success. It was a hard thing to do. He found a job and went to work for the firm with all the concentration he had brought to studying.

Kevin was four years old when the Blue Cross matured and we were able to have Susan. At the same time we bought our first house and John became less compulsive about his work.

Kevin's birth and the four years we spent together made him very special: the qualities he had made him even more special. He was quick, verbal, funny and interested in serious discussions. He was a good companion for me but not for John who did not know how to approach him. Once, when Kevin was eight, I drew John's attention to his needs for male companionship and John went right to work on it. He camped with the scouts, he helped Kevin build models, he tried to interest Kevin in hammers and nails. He made the most of what they had in common but it was never easy, as it was with our second son, Paul.

Kevin suffered all the overemphasis on behavior and accomplishments which firstborns suffer. Looking back, it seems to me that he also survived the period of my growing up . . . for I changed very much between the time of his birth and his entry into high school. In part this was the simple discovery that children can grow up pretty much on their own and that their selves were more theirs than my responsibility. I was able to enjoy Paul and Susan with much more freedom. Kevin still carries a great burden of seriousness.

When I think of Kevin's childhood, I see it all in terms of trying to instill in him more self-confidence. He was serious, he was fat, he had sticking-out teeth and he had, ingrained, a habit of facing straight up to every problem. He had great courage. He still has.

This mother, in a highly perceptive and articulate way, expresses some themes I have encountered with many mothers I have known in my more than twenty years as a child psychiatrist. First, she remembers the biological and medical details of her child's birth and the feelings she had during the experience. She had a hard time. There were complications. She had no emotional support from her own family, who were far away in America. In addition, there was the story of her mother-in-law who ruined her chances for more children by avoiding doctors for too long. Kevin's father John was preoccupied and exhausted by the need to study and get ahead. There was very little money. And her husband had to find a way to avoid repeating the situation of his own birth, the oft-told tale of "the complications" which made him the only child.

Out of this story of stress, difficulties and obstetrical troubles, the mother concludes, "I did not feel I had done a very good job." As in many such situations I have heard about, the mother felt she had something to make up for, a "poor job" to rectify. Because of her husband's great efforts to set up his career and the family's future, she had lots of time with Kevin, almost as an only parent. She even recalls that she later had to remind John that Kevin needed fathering. John needed, of course, to learn to be a father just as she needed to learn to be a mother. As always, they learned on the firstborn child. "You often burn the first pancake," one mother said. As usual, this mother was more deeply involved first. She had to give birth to the baby, and his well-being became a vital matter to her.

This leads to two important observations which arise from her self-awareness: "Kevin suffered all the over-emphasis on behavior and accomplishments which first-borns suffer," and also, *"Their selves were more theirs than my responsibility."*

Especially when birth has been hard, especially when it is a first experience, and even more when the situation gives all the responsibility to the mother, the early pattern of seeing the child's very existence and development as Mother's responsibility is very hard to break. Many a mother feels that she alone gives the child life and character, that every bit of behavior and every accomplishment has meaning in terms of whether she is "doing a good job" as a mother and a woman. Not every mother looks it all over later on and sees that her passionate involvement, fully appropriate and needed at the time of birth and in infancy, can become a terrible problem to her son or daughter as adulthood draws near. The new adult *must*, as part of his or her development, feel personal responsibility for his or her own identity. By making choices in the world of careers, love partner, life-style and values, the young adult begins to find out who he or she is. If, meanwhile, Mother still experiences this young adult as a project of her own, on which she has "done a poor job" or even "a good job," this will make the problem of separation and individuation very difficult for the child/young adult. *Needing* to prove one's own individuality, *needing* to take responsibility for one's own decisions and path, the young person will fight to remove any barriers. If your mother still acts as though she owns you, you are inwardly driven to prove to her and to yourself that she does not. This battle can lead to extreme and, in the end, self-destructive actions in the name of self-definition. It is far better when a mother, like this one, discerns that in the end children "pretty much grow up on their own" and take responsibility for themselves.

How can mothers help themselves let their children grow up their own way? Basically by keeping in touch with their own human needs as the children grow toward adulthood, by taking responsibility for the rechanneling of their own energy. As adolescents mature, mothers need to become more independent of them through interesting work, friend and colleague relationships and knowing how to enjoy their own lives.

All the above applies to fathers as well, at least those fathers who have become very emotionally involved with their growing children in the early years. Many fathers actually do not ever become very close with their children. But for those who do, it can be very hard to let go and face the fact that the child is an adult now. Fathers often use

money or the withholding of money as the power medium
to express who is in charge.

Of course, if the mother's and father's own love relationship has grown apace, if there is still interest in each
other and desire to spend time together, it helps im-
measurably. Thus, some fortunate couples can transfer
emotions back from the children toward each other and
still feel fully alive as the grown children move out and
onward into their own lives. But these days, this situation
seems to be unusual. Often the departure of the children,
whose needs and problems have provided the energy focus
that held the family together, leaves an emptiness between
the mother and father, who are now aware that they are
no longer interested in each other. Divorce can come at
this moment. Many family crises I have been called on
to deal with are like this: the young adult child is kept a
child too long in order to hold the family together, because
the mother and father don't love each other anymore.

Kevin got married. He and Sandra had been living
together for over a year, working out together the questions of whether to get married, and what kind of couple
relationship they wanted. Sandra had been in therapy,
resolving some of her own personal questions, and Kevin
also got into therapy. After one postponement because
Kevin didn't feel ready, they decided to marry. They wrote
their own wedding service with the help of an understanding minister their own age. The ceremony was small, just
family and a few friends. It was held on "neutral territory" in neither family's home. Here are some quotations
from it:

MINISTER: *Kevin and Sandra welcome you this evening.
In your presence and in the presence of the spirit
which each of us carries in part, they wish to make
the uniting of their two lives and their two visions a
matter of record and a matter for celebration.*

Within and between themselves Sandra and Kevin

are already married; their life together has continued intermittently for two years. But only recently have their souls let them know the mystery of their commitment, the depth of that commitment—so long a secret to them both. They wish you to hear and to feel so that in your world and in God's world, they shall be as one.

KEVIN: . . . *My secret is that in Sandra and myself, I have discovered a large number of links. Somehow our visions, abilities, needs and fears have combined in a strong and vital way, which makes the whole of our life so much greater than were our lives apart.*

To ignore this fact (although I have tried) is impossible and reckless since great harm could come of not feeling our joining for what it is already—a bonding, a connecting, indeed a marriage.

Now that I am sure of this knowledge, it must be proclaimed, for proclaiming our marriage strengthens it with other people's understanding and with their good wishes.

I do, therefore, ask for your understanding and your good wishes.

SANDRA: . . . *In my mind, as in Kevin's, we are already married. My commitment to him resides deep within me. Why then am I formally, legally, and publicly marrying Kevin? I am doing so because I feel that such an act will enhance my life and his—separately and together—and will put me in touch with my own deep feelings.*

KEVIN: *A wedding is, in part, preparation for having children. Looking towards the days when we will be parents, moves us to look at the days when we were our parents' children, and to recognize the change that marriage makes in the relationship between our parents and ourselves.*

SANDRA: *You, our parents, . . . gave us our growth. As we are a couple, you continue to be the earth in which our roots are planted. Now that the oak of our relationship has passed the first few hard winters and is strong enough to survive, we have not lost the need for nourishment from our roots. We indeed hope our bonds with you will grow stronger as our marriage grows and strengthens.*

KEVIN: *Yet, there must be change in the nuture we receive from you because the food which nourished us as children no longer sustains us. As you grew up and separated from your parents, you chose the path which was for you a responsible life. As children we learned of the path which was your life. As was the case with you, we also have diverged from your path to find what we consider a responsible life. Just as you were not required to follow your parents' ways, do not ask us to follow yours.*

SANDRA: *Our path is not always straight and true; we can get lost. Sometimes a signpost is needed; if we can come to you at that point and ask for direction, our bond will be stronger.*

KEVIN: *As we feel the possibility of coming to you for direction, we also hope that you can see the possibility of our assistance.*

The travels which are your lives have a long time to run as of yet, and as we face new choices, so do you.   There may come a time that you can come to us and ask directions in a clear voice. We will be glad to share what we know.

Then Kevin and Sandra turned toward their parents and asked them:

KEVIN: *"Will you, Elizabeth and Martin, add your support to our union, give us space as we explore and direction as we ask?*

E & M: *We will.*

SANDRA: *Will you, Louise and John, add your support to our union, give us space as we explore and direction as we ask?*

L & J: *Gladly.*

* * *

I attended the wedding. When I heard Kevin and Sandra ask their parents these vital questions, I was moved to tears. They didn't want assurances of continued care, they wanted to know that they could stand in the world with their parents *as equals*—not only wanting the right to come home for guidance and advice, but also wanting to be available *themselves* as a new adult married couple, should their parents want or need their help. "Separate but but equal" is the theme.

Kevin's mother wrote me some of her thoughts and feelings after the wedding:

Since the wedding Kevin and Sandra have seemed much happier, much gayer and less prickly than they were before. This makes me feel good; I like to see Kevin happy. Quite honestly, I do not feel able to project his future life and make any predictions. . . . I accept his control of it and decisions about it.

I feel very separated from him at this moment. In part, I guess, this is normal separation and perfectly acceptable. In another part, I mourn the fact that he has not discussed with us at any time his feelings and wedding plans, but assumed our cooperation and otherwise ignored us. We feel like facilities. My only definite expectation and hope about my children once they are grown and away, which is the point of all this, is that they should be friends to us, available for conversation and humor and education. . . . Two years ago, Kevin and Sandra gave me emotional support in a bad time, and it is something I treasure and hope will happen again when I need it.

My only conversation with Kevin about the wedding was initiated by me when he was trapped under his car repairing something and I was able to ask him the questions I wanted to about why was he getting married, instead of living with Sandra and was able to express to him my sense of him as a special person. For me this was important. I have no idea what it meant to Kevin.

One of the questions I asked Kevin under the car was why they did not leave this geographical area since inde-

pendence would be easier to establish somewhere else. His answer was that their respective jobs depended on word of mouth, etc. It is said that independence must be won and cannot be given. I also expressed to him my sense that it is more difficult for the artist than for others to find food for self-esteem and ego and that I was concerned about where he found it. He replied that he found it where he teaches and in his work . . . and, I should think, in Sandra.

No matter whence, he has found his place to live and his partner. I look to the future where I trust, and have a deep faith, that his creativity will increase and be recognized by more people, where I hope he will be able to be my friend in both joy and need. I admire him as a human being and am proud to be his mother.

Aware of her mixed feelings, feeling in one part of herself her hurt that she was not consulted about the wedding plans, that she and John were "facilities," still this mother has made the vital step—she has given up her little boy. He is no longer her responsibility; he is his own man now. Facing the grief over the loss of Kevin as a child, she feels the joy of a new relationship with Kevin as friend and equal.

2. "Who has been sitting in my chair?"

A woman in her late forties, mother of four sons, tells this story:

I could say a few things about my parents first. My parents were a primary unit and I was definitely second in line. (Also an only child.) For a long time I felt badly about that, but now I value it. I did feel my parents were not accessible—my father was quiet although we had political discussions (he was a rabid Republican). He died when I was a senior in college.

I was loathing my mother when I went away to school. She was very volatile—didn't keep anything in. My mother was frank in a narcissistic way, though I wasn't encouraged to ask questions. I value her expressiveness now, and though we still don't really talk, we communicate by sharing an activity such as cooking or sewing together.

Concerning my children, I think one of the most outstanding experiences was a few months before Walt was twenty-two years old. I had been shopping for groceries and came home in the early afternoon. I looked out on the porch and there was Walt and his girlfriend Marcy sitting in the deck chairs my husband Sam and I always sit in. My younger sons Dick and Peter were bringing them drinks and just kind of fussing over them. My first reaction was, "Who has been sitting in my chair?" I felt terribly displaced, as though I had been catapulted into instant grandmotherhood. I was jealous and irrationally tearful. I realized in part that I hadn't really heard much about Marcy, that Walt's courtship with her had gone on without much participation from me. I hadn't been let in on the process. I know that when Walt had had love problems earlier, he had gone to his father and assumed Sam had told me about it, so that afterward we could make open allusions to it though we had never really talked. His relationship with Marcy is a very classic bind— he cares for her and wants her to be there (on tap almost) but does not want to take on the responsibility of a family (she has a child) at this point in his life. He still is very involved with boyish things, cars, clothes and so on.

I didn't feel much of a wrench when Walt went away to college. I did feel awful when we took my second son, Daniel, to boarding school. He left home at thirteen, and as we left him sitting forlornly on his bunk bed at school, I felt as though I was abandoning him. I remember having a fight with Sam that night—I couldn't respond lovingly to him because I was still too wrapped up in being Dan's mother. I knew he would never come home the same— and he never did, though boarding school was good for him and soon things were all right.

The boys, with the exception of Daniel, don't really have much to fight against as a means of growing up. Ex-

*cept for Dan, they don't have anger to propel them out:
in fact, leaving for them is a wrench because it is so nice
at home. An example is when we "kicked" Walt out of
the house at age twenty. He had left college after one
semester and was hanging around the house, fixing his
car and drinking beer with his buddies. We talked and
tried to help him find a job and a place to live. He felt
he had to have one to get the other—of course, a never-
ending circular snare. Finally we gave him an ultimatum—
out on your own!—and he burst into tears. "Why can't I
pay you rent and stay? I like it here." We both felt so
badly that we stood in the kitchen and cried.*

*The boys each have their special way of manipulating,
in order to get what they want. They are dependent on us
financially (except Walt), and if they want more than their
allowance, they can work around the house. Sometimes
we have to remind them that we aren't money machines—
for instance, when Dan makes the announcement, "I
need . . ." Dick is the most dependent and comes around
to talk and for assurances. He nags to get what he wants
and eventually I will give in so that he will go away. Dan
also nags—he drills—and will play Sam and me off
against each other. I will sometimes give him what he
wants to shut him up. Peter—the young genius who needs
so much—(money for supplies for his projects) just quietly
"suffers" until he gets what he wants. He knows I am completely adoring of his talent and have a hard time saying
no. He will bring something he has just finished to me and
hope I get the right idea. Walt also "suffers" and is
silently reproachful.*

*For me I find that when I am lonely or feel separated
from Sam I use the boys' love as a crutch for comfort. I
know that their love is largely uncritical. I think this has
led to at least three of the boys being deeply tied to me
emotionally and that it is going to take some doing to end
the Oedipal lock-in they have. I also tend to get naggy—
sometimes in the morning I would get after them; but
now I don't get up, and they manage very well getting
their own breakfast. I also keep after them to clean up*

their rooms, and when they answer, "But, Moooother, it is my room," I tell them that in this commune my word goes—that I can't have the rugs in their rooms cleaned if the cleaning man can't find them.

I don't think I would have answered these questions this way fifteen years ago—things have changed and grown much better as we have gotten older and wiser. For one thing, I felt quite martyred caring for four little boys all the time because Sam was so very busy and gone much of the time. And when he was home, he often needed a great deal of attention himself—times he would come in the door obviously just shot. I have often wished he had had more time with the boys to play sports or go to games with them (he hates ball games) or do things with them separately. There have been times when he has taken one boy because it was so obviously needed. But Sam is "father" to about eighty people at work and it makes it very hard for him. Our time together is limited and overprogrammed.

Things have greatly evolved for us as a family, however. We shared and faced my recent illness together as a family and some of the results have been dramatically important. Dan overnight turned from a selfish little boy to a considerate young man. In the past we tended to conceal big problems, but we talk about them more openly as a family now and we have done it consciously. I would say things have greatly evolved.

I do worry quite a bit about the boys' "careers." I worry about what they will be. I was extremely upset when Walt dropped out of school. I worry that he will be ill-equipped to do much of anything. I suppose I feel very traditional about education and I also realize that the reason Sam is able to do much of what he does and make an impact is because of his Harvard credentials. I wanted Sam to lean on Walt a little more, but I trust that Walt will eventually come to a decision about his life, and when he wants something badly enough he will go after it. The other boys like school, so we shall see about them. It is important to me that they are able to do what they want to with their lives.

*I would like, for example, for the future, to keep this
house for the grandchildren. I am jealous of pregnant
women a little and realize that that part of my productive
life is over. It has been important to me to have more
than just children, so that time away from my family was
not time on my hands. Still, it would be nice to have a
growing family gather for holidays after they have begun
their own lives. The older we all get the more interesting
and together as a family we become.*

Here is another mother who is deeply aware of her own
feelings about her children. Not denying her own feelings
of jealousy of Walt's girlfriend or of loss and grief when
Dan went off to boarding school, she has been able to
retain her authority on the home scene, keep close to her
husband and not only let her sons go when it seems best
for them, but also, as in Walt's case, to *make* them go
when it seems necessary. At the same time she has managed to be there for them emotionally whether they're
home or not. As with the first mother I quoted, she *knows*
her own feelings and needs well enough to follow and
meet them, and thus she doesn't need to hang on to her
children because they are all she's got and all she has
ever been involved with.

She got a shock seeing Walt and Marcy sitting in the
chairs of honor—but she quickly figured out why she was
upset and didn't dump rage or retaliation on the young
couple, which would have estranged Walt from her. She
is aware of the "Oedipal lock-in" most of her sons tend to
have with her; she seeks their uncritical love when her
husband is not giving her enough, but she resists pamper-
ing them and tying them to her by indirect devices the
way many mothers do when they feel needy.

In many family situations I have worked with professionally, it becomes obvious that many parents' criticism
of their grown-up children's values and life-styles is, in
part, a displacement of anger. The parents are angry inside
because they feel rejected and abandoned to lives that
feel empty and sterile to them. These parents feel like

abandoned children, but one can't express this openly in our society. "My children have left me and now I've got nothing that matters." Mothers particularly, because they tend to have made a career of their families, have retirement depressions when children go away, so they may clutch and hang on. This leads to squirming and kicking for freedom on the part of the child. This in turn leads to more power moves by the parent, and so on. Such struggles can go on well into the children's thirties, even forties, and can be the main events in the entire interaction of a family. One thirty-seven-year-old woman invited her parents for Christmas and allowed them to meet a couple of her under-thirty friends—a young male college dropout searching for something in life to interest him, and a young woman in training to become a psychologist. The atmosphere was so close and relaxed among these young people, the grandchildren and the daughter, that the parents felt terribly uptight and out of place. Unable to deal with these feelings openly, they spent the holiday working around the house, tidying and cleaning up everything.

"Mother, why don't you relax? I had the house cleaned for you and now you're doing it again! Come sit and talk," said her daughter. But her parents wouldn't let themselves be near these "hippies" that their daughter obviously liked. By the end of the day the mother had declared that her daughter's life "repulsed" her and was unhealthy. The visit ended in the middle of the night.

Parents of grown-up children have every right to disagree with their children's values and ways of life, of course, and to express these feelings. But if this is still happening so violently when the child is thirty-seven, there is usually more to it than simple value differences across the generation gap. This woman remembered that the same issue dated back to her teens; her parents violently rejected her friends and her goals in life, "except when they were just like their ways of seeing and doing things. *Then* they loved me." Twenty years later these parents are still working on the same question: Can they love their daughter *as she is,* not as they want her to be? They haven't been able to see how their own needs are still forcing them to object to their daughter's life-style. Unlike the first two mothers in this chapter, they are probably not going to become friends and equals with their grown child. All three will then miss the love and closeness they need.

In a couple, one feels the continuous interaction of needs—for as long as both still love each other. Marriage partners or those who live together as lovers must face the duality—what do I *need* my partner to be for me, and what is my partner *really?* Adjustments are made continuously. When one feels that his or her partner ceases to provide enough satisfaction for one's needs, something has to happen—a demand is made, a need expressed. If it can't be met, some of the energy that went into the loving interaction is withdrawn.

But partners are not going to live forever with their adolescent children. Sometimes during adolescence *both* parents and children must make preparations for withdrawal of most of the loving energy that has been invested in their relationship. As the rebellions and voyages of adolescence signal the child's struggle to withdraw this energy from the "loved child" role and reinvest it in a self-defined life-style, so the parents must start withdrawing energy from the "loving parent" role and reinvesting it in a life-style and identity that are no longer that of "active parent." If this process doesn't happen *bilaterally,* the young adult may have to wrench free, leaving a lot of hurt and pain behind. Or if he or she can't pull free alone, he or she may remain too dependent too long, at a cost to his or her own freedom and self-esteem. As this interview makes clear, some parents do not recognize in time how hard it is for them to let go of their children, especially parents who haven't ever established a strong sense of their own identity.

3. "My children give me more advice than I give them."

A psychiatrist father, a widower:

I think it's wonderful to see kids grow up and me always remaining the same.

It's a quip that I often use, but I feel somehow there is a lot of truth in it. I don't feel as though I have ever treated my kids as "children"; I have tried to treat them as little people. So it is difficult to remember turning points. They are all three (two boys and a girl) married, with children of their own, and it has been a long while since I have been anything besides Grandpa. It was good fortune for me that my children were growing and almost grown before the drug culture hit. Their schooling was satisfactory. They seemed to have minimal trouble during their teens because they were each well liked in their way, and because my wife was the kind of woman she was, they would hang around our yard or house and we almost always knew what was going on. The kids in the neighborhood were fundamentally decent—some had difficulties later on while they were at college, but when they were in high school these things hadn't come up.

My wife and I had our disagreements or fights in a special room—not the bedroom because that was a sacred room—but also not in front of the children. Yet they always knew something was up and would ask, "Are you okay?" I told them what I have since told my patients many times: "Anger is not evil, but is a spur to problem-solving." We had a very congenial relationship the twenty years we were together—I can see in my daughter a lot of my wife—she handles her husband in the same breezy way that my wife handled me. I was the boss, but she managed everything very well. I thank her profoundly for much of how my children are today—she gave them lots of time for laughter. But, let me see. My oldest son was always quite competitive with me—and for many years we were able only to swap accomplishments—he al-

ways showing his latest and wanting to know about mine. Then one summer about eight years ago, he beat me in a game of tennis for the first time. As were were walking off the court, he put his arm on my shoulder and said, "You played a good game, Dad." As if all the times I had won my game wasn't so good . . . but I knew that he felt more my equal than ever before. Now that I look back on our relationship, I feel grateful that I was as certain of myself professionally as I was because I didn't have to subconsciously prove my worth to my children and felt for the most part lighthearted about how I did things. I also included them when I did any writing—they played with the tapes while I dictated—sometimes I would hear their singing later. My oldest is a political scientist and we send each other papers or articles and I feel he has added a great deal to my knowledge of the world—it pleases me. His passage from child to adult was the smoothest, I believe, of the three.

My second son did not finish college—he has always been the practical one of the family. Early on he knew more about how everything worked than I and to this day I can hear myself or one of the others saying, "Go ask Teddy." I know that the year he dropped out of Yale was agonizing for him—he got some help which went on for a year or so—and emerged with the understanding that he felt angry with his mother because she died while he was still young—and because he felt she had favored his older brother. (Which may have been somewhat true.) Children have an enormous capacity for accurate observation—and they aren't often wrong about these impressions, no matter how much someone might deny the truth. He is now the most successful financially of all of us. He and I have less of a colleague relationship—it is less "easy" than what I share with his brother, but I feel an underlying, deep emotional tie that I don't think we could talk about.

My relationship with my daughter has been awkward from time to time because she was only sixteen when her mother died. I leaned on her quite a lot in the early days, married on the rebound and was divorced. I think she was forced to grow up in a big hurry, and missed some of the tender times that I would have wanted for her. I think also (partly because she has caught me at it) that I placed a premium on her being grown up which did not allow her to come at it in her own time. Only recently has she begun to be angry about that and I do understand that it was wrong of me. It has left her with what seems like an unquenchable longing for she doesn't know what. She lives in Boston and we see each other more often than the others—I like her husband and child very much. She gives me daughterly advice on my lady friends and soothes me over when something has gone wrong. Now that I think of it—my children give me more advice than I give them. I wonder is it because they have braved the world and know more about it than I do now? They didn't go through the war, nor experience the holocaust as I did— but somehow our problems today are different, and people are different. I still go to work every day (I love what I do) so I am still very involved in things away from my family. I suppose that both interests and relieves them.

This thoughtful father found out a number of things from his relationship with his three children. He could accept that his second son was not going to be so easy and "colleague-like" with him as the first son, and understood that dropping out of college was "agonizing for *him*," more than any pain or loss to his parents. How often parents take it as *their* loss when a child leaves college, not seeing the struggle from the other side!

This father also sees how his own neediness after his wife's death took some of the childhood away from his daughter and affected her character. As I commented on earlier parents' interviews, parents' needs (in this case, his need for the daughter to replace her dead mother in caring for him) often make it hard for grown children to actualize themselves. But here, the father sees how he leaned on her heavily and accepts her anger about it as justified. Because he is absorbed in his work, and she in her new family, the situation has straightened out. He is able to let go of his grown children's lives.

There is a theme in the comments of this father and the two mothers I wrote about before him: taking responsibility for the ways in which our own characters and life decisions affect the developing characters of our children. This father sees how his needing to lean on his daughter after her mother died was an imposition on her freedom, a high-priority demand on her ability to love and give before she was fully a woman. He accepts that her anger over it is justified. The first mother accepts the fact that she overdoted on her son's every act and word, under the stress of the difficult life conditions around his birth and early years when she herself was lonely: "almost an only parent." The second mother in this chapter saw the threat of her closeness to her oldest son, recognized her jealousy of his girlfriend and had the guts to press him to leave home despite her own wanting to keep him close.

None of us can bring up children uninfluenced by our own weaknesses and mistakes. The story of any family is that *all* members pay dues for *all* members' problems. The essential difference between the healthy family and the sick one is the extent to which each member is *aware* of what is going on and thus can accept responsibility for what he or she is doing to each other. In the sickest families I have known, people hurt each other and deny each other the love and concern they need, but all the time no one is facing the truth. Many of the young adults whose interviews I presented in Part Three come from such families. In these families there are people who are always right and others who are always wrong. No one feels heard or understood.

Parents may read this book seeking how to be perfect parents for adolescents, to make sure they will become friends once they have grown up and left home. No one can be a perfect parent. There is no magic method for parents to follow; what they need is *self-awareness,* constant looking at themselves to see how they are affecting those around them. Parents who create and maintain an atmosphere of openness will always hear from their spouse and their children how they are affecting them. A very useful way to keep up on what kind of person you are is simply to listen! In one family I know, the parents set up weekly "feelings meetings" in which everyone was encouraged to raise any issues, or gripes. Everyone was guaranteed he or she would be heard out and not judged or outranked. After a few initial complaints that having weekly meetings was "arbitrary" or "phony," everyone participated and it made a great difference in everyone's feelings of being understood. A sense of closeness developed.

By contrast, in families where the parents teach a style of authoritarian dealing with issues, the only way out for the children is to crash their way out angrily, full of unrevealed and unresolved feelings. As with Henry and Peter in chapter 5, working out these feelings in order to become an adult can be a very difficult and long process. Even when parents are not cruel but simply too weak emotionally to face their own difficulties, the effect can paralyze the children. If the work of understanding who we are and what we do to each other is not done within the family, it will need to be done afterward, very likely in therapy. When I assess the health of a family, I ask myself, "How open, how aware?"

4. "I feel a deep-down sadness that my son and I are so much at odds."

Father, an engineer:

I have one child—a son who is now twenty-nine. He has been married and divorced (no children) and is currently living with a woman. I don't know what their plans are, but they seem to be muddling through somehow.

I have many mixed feelings about Mark—sometimes I am surprised when I look at him and remember that he was ever small. He acts the same way he always has in many respects. He has a manner which is quite mature and even somewhat somber, yet he is so inefficient in doing things—it took him years to finish graduate school—and I still don't know what he plans to do with himself. (I don't think he does, either.) This creates one of the major clashes between us. I simply cannot understand how he can go on day after day piddling around at this "art business" (he likes to make sculptures) and not take on any responsibility for his financial security. I often wonder if he has in the back of his mind that he will inherit everything since he is the only child, and therefore doesn't really have to work for anything himself.

He says this isn't true—that his "real vocation" is to be an artist and if he must be poor to do it, then, by God, he will. What he doesn't seem to understand is that he isn't poor and that his estimation of the situation is very, very unrealistic. You see, we have been always available in a pinch; my wife is always "giving him a helping hand" (she thinks I don't notice, but of course I do), and even though he has paid his own way through summer and extra work, he has never had to face anything really big.

I grew up in genuine poverty; we often did not have enough to eat because my father was killed in an accident while he was working, leaving my mother with six children. I used to look at the big houses around where I lived and swear that someday I would have one of my own. I worked my way through school, and worked very, very hard afterwards; now I have gotten what I want. I suppose the fact that I have had to work so hard for my dreams has made me intolerant of sloppiness. I really do not understand the workings of my son's mind. He isn't childish exactly; I think the best way I could describe it is that he is unrealistic.

We have had, certainly, many discussions about this. It usually begins when someone in the family makes a stray remark and a little scrapping begins. For example: My wife made a comment about the amnesty thing. I've forgotten exactly, but she said that there should be forgiveness all around

—if we excuse the draft dodgers and incorporate them back into American life, then it is also a good idea to stop pursuing the Watergate people, and incorporate them back into American life—everyone was just doing what they thought was right. My son says that the older generation (me) did very "important work" in creating a materially comfortable world, and that it is up to his generation to make it spiritually pure or something like that. Does this mean that just because someone belongs to the older generation and breaks the law he goes to jail, and if a member of the younger generation breaks the law, he is trying to purify things? I don't buy it.

I don't think my gripe is with Mark's being "an artist"— I love to work with wood and make beautiful pieces myself. My gripe is that I don't believe that you get what you need and want for free. I work on my "art" after I have made sure that my family eats well and lives well. I also think the world could use some cleaning up. There is nothing I hate more than the incredible ugliness of the city— I think the way we have exploited the environment is madness—I grow my own vegetables every summer— have been for years. I think the "pop" culture stinks and has no depth. But I don't believe that the way things get better is by living off of someone else's work.

If I am perfectly frank with you, I suppose I am a little jealous of the freedom my son has to move and explore. I wish I had more time in my life for it—I do believe it is important. But that is not the bulk of my disapproval, I am certain.

My son and I are peers only in a limited way. It is very difficult to say this, but I don't respect my son right now. I hope against hope that I will be able to. I can't, of course, ever prohibit anything he does—I haven't for ten years. I try not to give him any advice unless he asks for it; and he does ask about specific matters occasionally (tires, insurance, tools). Most of all right now, I feel a deep-down sadness that my son and I are so much at odds. I do like many things about him. He is basically a good person; he is smart, and I don't worry that he will ever get into

trouble. I secretly believe that if he should marry again the
gaps between us will close somewhat—but I guess that
doesn't leave room for me to change.

This forthright and outspoken father underlines one very
current issue between parents and grown-up children: the
huge change in values and life-styles over the last thirty
years. This father's son simply does not think, does not
live, in a way that makes sense to his father. Most parents
are fully, even painfully aware of differences in values and
life-styles between themselves and their children. And
most parents feel sad and even angry over these differences. Fortunately, this father sees that he can't prohibit
his son from anything, and avoids giving advice unless
asked.

One technique I devised for parents and children whose
values and life-styles are very different is this: Either
parent or adult child may want to talk about an experience or a feeling. This person asks the other:

"I want to tell you about something that happened to
me (or that I am feeling). Is that all right?"
Listener: *Either "Yes" or "Not now. How about this*
evening when I have more time?" or (conceivably), "I
don't want to listen to anybody now. Can I let you know
when I feel like it?"
If the listener has agreed to listen, the initiator proceeds
to get the experience or feeling off his or her chest. There
is an understanding in this technique that response must
be asked for and permitted by the initiator:
Listener: *"Hearing that story gives me some reactions.*
Do you want to hear them?"
Initiator: *"Yes," or "No," or whatever he or she feels up*
to.

In short, this technique is designed to let people communicate experiences and feelings to each other while
maintaining some control over the feared possibility that
the listener (one's parent or one's adult child) will respond

with harsh criticism or judgment. Thus this game allows
revelation *without* retaliation. Surprisingly, after prac-
ticing this for a while, the parent or the grown child
realizes that one *can* actually hear the other's feelings and
opinions *without* attacking them. Knowing that this can
happen seems to sensitize people to the fact that they have
been in an attack-counterattack relationship and this sometimes makes new and less retaliatory styles of response
begin to be used.

All this boils down to the fact that more and more
young people are growing up to think and live more and
more differently from their parents, and hassling them
for it is going to do no good at all. This father has recognized that.

5. "It is so hard for me not to be able to take her unhappiness away."

Dancer and mother of two grown daughters:

*I have two lovely daughters with whom I have been
able to establish a pleasing and, I think, comfortable (for
all of us) friendship.*

*My older daughter, Jane, was the easiest—paradoxically
—because she was with me during my most tumultuous
years early in her life—she was born when I was nineteen,
and emotionally very young. I was later divorced and had
much to go through, and I think her early years reflected
this. She was (and is) quiet, shy sometimes, extremely com-
petent and conservative. She has a great awareness of her
own need for security.*

*I think that one of the most outstanding times was when
we bought a pony when the girls were in the third and
fourth grades. This pony was a fantasy come true—almost.
It turned out to be a very feisty and hard-to-handle pony.
It would bite or stand on your foot or sidle over to you
and lean four hundred pounds against you, and squash
you against the side of the stall. When the girls would get
on to ride, it would just flop over. We all were afraid of*

this pony at first and had to learn to be firm; the girls didn't have the physical strength to fight with, so they had to discover other strengths. To show who was boss was very hard to learn, but they did. Also they had to learn to deal with anger, and they would become rightfully angry with this pony which they also dearly loved. What to do? The experience was fantastically enriching and important, their first experience at learning to control something bigger than themselves.

When Jane was thirteen or fourteen she became really interested in dance. She began taking courses at the conservatory where I taught. We lived in a very rural area and when she reached high school she decided she wanted to study dance seriously. The rural high school was wonderful and easygoing, but did not have anything adequate for what she wanted. So we arranged with them to have her finish all her classes before noon, and then she could go into the city in the afternoon to dance. At first she went one day a week; this was not easy because she had to catch a bus and then a subway, dance and come home the same way. By the time she was fifteen, she went every afternoon, and when she learned to drive she took my car up the expressway. It was for her a way of finding her own power, something she could do all on her own. I was worried about how I could teach the girls caution without frightening them. I must say that they both were very cooperative. We made a contract—and I told them that I would trust if they would abide—when there was an issue like hitchhiking, we both said (my husband and I) that we were unalterably opposed to it, and to pot, because it was illegal. If they chose to do those things, it was without our permission—that decision was their own— we would grieve but we would not feel guilty.

I think it is one of the hardest things for a parent to learn WHEN *to relinquish authority over their children. It is different with each child, different in other parts of the country and even in different years, historically. My older daughter took on responsibility very well. I can't remember when it was quite, but I began to notice that she*

*mixed her "I ams" with her "May I's" until finally there
were no more "May I's" left.*

*With both of them, my most predominant way of
holding and perhaps intruding (though it was only from
genuine care and concern) was a "Why don't you?" This
was not exactly a "You must" but some sort of manipulation just the same. With my older daughter it came in the
form of, "Why don't you study Russian literature?" or,
"Why don't you become your dorm representative—I
think that would be really exciting!" She didn't pay much
attention to me. Then I got another idea— "Why don't you
become a brain surgeon, you have such delicate hands, you
are an excellent problem solver!" I think I pressed her
several times and finally she said to me, "I could become a
Russian literature scholar, I could become my dorm representative, and if I wanted to I could even become a
brain surgeon—I don't doubt it—and YOU would be very
happy." I said, "You're right, I'll take care of my own
happiness."*

*She was always very good at telling me when to fuck off
in a very nice way. When she was young I thought she had
serious problems—because she was so shy and cautious.
Sometime when she was about eight I began to accept her
as a whole person and I ceased to worry. She has emerged
as her own person very strongly. There was one time when
things between us snapped and they have always been
different since. She was thirteen or fourteen and told me
she wanted to practice ballet at the bar every night and
would I help. One night I told her to move in a particular
way and she resisted. Things got pretty wild; finally, something came over me and I said to her, "I know I am your
mother, but I am also a dancer and I know ballet. We
can discuss your feelings about me as your mother later;
right now I am your teacher—point your toe and shut up."
I think at that moment she respected me. I think too that
she had been unconsciously testing me. Something now
became free and clear between us. There had never been
much goo, but whatever there was, was gone. She can say
no strongly and readily to me, and will never say yes*

unless she really feels it. This enables me to ask out-rageous things of her. I can say no to her as well. This has been very, very important.

I don't want anything from her I am not getting; what is hard is that I know she is unhappy right now and that it is none of my business. It is so hard for me not to be able to take her unhappiness away. She is in Nebraska studying to become a veterinarian and it is a desert there. She used to go to the museum weekly, alone—something I could never do—and she worked for three years after college to assure herself (not us) that she could do so. She has great inner resourcefulness and I respect her so much.

My second daughter is or rather was, different. She was a wonderful, exuberant, abundant child—the opposite of her sister when young. She was simply a pleasure to look at—she was easy. When she was angry, you knew it, when she had anything on her mind you knew it—she just said it, wide open. She is still that way. Adolescence hit her with a big boom. To be a trusting, loving creature in the early sixties was not always to your advantage in making your way. She very early made the decision that she wanted to be an actress—she was always putting on a display (the older daughter was tidy—and often she and I both were in the background ironing at the last minute, dashing here or there, thinking to be of help). She is enormously creative and imaginative. With her I really messed up. The way it happened was quite innocuous and subtle—but I was always "Why don't you?"ing her—she brought all her problems to me and I always had a helpful (and pretty good, too) suggestion. At times when I should have taken the time to teach or urge her to do something, I found it easier to do it myself. But she needed to do those things to give herself a sense of rootedness in reality. (The pony experience was very good for her, too—a real fantasy come true—with all the pony shit that followed. It wasn't enough, of course.) She had a deep sense that she was not able to take care of herself. When adolescence hit, she would start in the morning: "What shall I wear?" I would answer, "Why don't you . . . ?" and

*she would try it. "It looks awful." Same with her hair,
or school assignments, any number of small, daily decisions. What began to happen to me is that I became
constantly a failure—why couldn't I solve this child's
problems? She left every little speck of detail to me. She
felt inept (though she was often successful) and would
have wide swings of contradictions. Finally, she asked if
she could see someone for some help. We agreed and she
paid half and we paid half. She really needed a third person. I spoke to the therapist once, but it was enough.
She told me I had to stop controlling, albeit a sweet and
delightful controlling. It wasn't helpful. It was very, very
hard for me to give it up. But the mornings came when
I would answer, "I'm sure there is something in your
closet—you have a wonderful imagination, you choose!"
She would press, and though it was hard, I would throw
it back. I got very strict about neatness. I became the firm
mother of a teen-ager and there were lots of battles. She
would often leap before looking, and oh, I worried. She
was afraid to take the "I am" step, and we would say, you
can't ask for your freedom, you have to take it.*

*She went to Europe on a grant from a foundation—she
is a superb movement teacher—and wrote the most de-
spairing letters, baring her soul; I am suicidal, and so on—
everything into the letters. I had to exercise my greatest
self-control to answer with lots of reassurance but no "Why
don't you's?" She pulled through beautifully.*

*The next year she went to London and had another dif-
ficult time—but she learned that year that she didn't
really want to be an actress because "I love people too
much." She is at home now—as an adult, I might add—
saving money to return to Europe to be with a man with
whom she has fallen in love.*

*I feel so happy that I have peopled my world with
people I adore, and am nourished by—I feel I have two
sisters now. We had a wonderful summer this last one—
doing things we dearly love—giggling in the bathroom together, showering, fixing our hair. It was joyous for me.*

*   *   *

I included this interview because it is so revealing of a kind of interaction so many parents and their children share—the power game of *who controls whom,* as played out here subtly between the mother and her second daughter. So often when an adolescent comes to a parent for advice over some trivial matter like: "What shall I wear? What courses shall I take this semester? Should I go to the dance with Bob or Ted?" it seems such a cozy thing for Mother to be helpful to her daughter, to share a decision here or there. But when this becomes a pattern, it can seduce the parent into staying parent long after it is wise to be parental. This mother even reached the point where she was feeling guilty: "Why couldn't I solve this child's problems?" A wise therapist awakened this mother's awareness to the fact that she was being drawn into her daughter's developmental problem: her reluctance to take responsibility for herself, and her dependence upon her mother's wisdom and resourcefulness to avoid the issue.

We are so used to seeing the reverse problem these days—children who not only don't ask for parents' advice, but wouldn't accept it no matter how good it might be. So this more seductive game goes on in many families almost unnoticed. Once again, this demonstrates the need for *self-awareness* on the part of the parent.

Let's suppose, though, that this mother were not so happy in her marriage and her work as a dance teacher. Like many mothers around forty, she might be feeling a loss of usefulness and purpose as a wife and mother, and might not have any skills that are interesting to her. Many mothers in this predicament are prey to the temptation to control their adolescent children a little longer, to make them need Mother. This seems to be a particular problem for divorced mothers who often turn their rejected needs to be loved and needed onto their children long after the children have stopped needing so much care.

Once the need for parents' advice and direction has gotten too strong, it is hard for adolescents to grow apart from their parents. Either they can't leave home or they get into messes which dump them back at home over and

over again. And once these overprotected young people
have finally moved out of the home, I have also seen how
hard it is for them to relate as equals with parents. As
one woman told me, "Whenever I'm around my parents
again for more than a day, I get paralyzed. I can't decide
anything. I feel like I was twelve years old on a rainy
Sunday, waiting for Mom and Pop to decide what we'd
do today. I have no identity near them."

6. "They are responsible for themselves—we are available to them."

A mother and father of three:

*I don't think we ever thought about what we ourselves
wanted from grown-up children. Oh, we did want them to
be happy and that sort of thing, and to be good citizens,
whatever the hell that means these days. But to want to
know them as people, to be friendly and enjoy them—
yes, to be nourished by their existence—we never thought
of it.*

*There are three—two boys, men—and a woman. They
are in their middle to late twenties and all real individuals.
The youngest has been a great heartache for us because he
has been deeply unhappy, still is. We have tried and tried
to help and get help in every way we know how but he
resists and it leaves us bewildered. He has such contradictions within him—he is utterly charming, handsome and
wildly unsure of himself. He mows through people like
there was no tomorrow, and yet they often remain his
friends, or at least open and loyal for years. He is a
musician though not very good, and loves nothing else
as much.*

*When he was a baby he was hilarious, darling, chubby
and born at a point when we (especially the two of us)
were settled and fairly relaxed with each other (we had
married at the end of WW II during difficult times). The
next ten years were very happy ones for us; we had the
usual family squabbles, and some difficulty making ends*

meet occasionally, but we had three healthy and lovely children and each other.

The turning point we remember (though you know how things are, there were probably signs before had we looked) was the year we moved to the East Coast. We left the children with their grandparents and went house hunting and second honeymooning that summer. When we came for them, we discovered that the youngest had begun to have terrible nightmares and what he called "terrible thoughts"—they being nothing more than thoughts about us in bed (making love). That in itself we understood—an awakening sexuality—but he was only ten years old and that we didn't understand. We probably would have let it go except that he began to develop grave difficulties in school: he stopped learning to read, he became terribly withdrawn and morbid, almost. Not sure what to do we talked with his teacher and she suggested a psychiatrist. What we eventually discovered is that he began puberty at a very early age, and that he probably wasn't emotionally ready for it. (Is anyone??) We were able to make a lot of headway that year, we thought, but the problems kept (and still do) reappearing in many different forms. He was often in trouble—sometimes with the law—and always feeling enormously guilty, always needing "to confess." This kind of thing has come and gone all through high school and college, and it is an agony for us.

We sent him to a high-quality private day school for his last two years of high school, and it helped him greatly, in his being able to believe he was as smart as he is and able to learn. It had a disastrous effect on him socially— we think—because he rubbed noses with children of famous parents, and has allowed most of their snobbery to rub off—on the one hand he wants to be very special, on the other he won't believe he already is—even the feedback from these same children doesn't manage to convince him of much.

He recently signed himself into a mental hospital in a neighboring town and has been there for several weeks.

We are at a loss as to what to do; he won't see a therapist because he thinks they are all "meat men." Yet he relies on us totally for money and support, and we are less and less able to take care of him. He doesn't seem to be able to hold a job—he quits or is fired after a few months. He won't return to school to get his degree; he floats from friend to friend, charming them into meals and shelter— a real gypsy. He is such an enigma. We ache for him, but it is getting more and more impossible to do anything helpful. It has been suggested that in some way we need him to be dependent on us as we are just past fifty years old, and ending our "productive years." I suppose anything could be the reason, but somehow we neither of us feel we want to keep "taking care of the children" anymore. We want time to ourselves—my husband, especially, has not had a chance to explore his interior—and having dependent children siphons off so much energy.

The older boy is quite different. What is it they say about middle children . . . they always seem to adapt?? In this case, it is strangely true. This child was a bundle, feisty, tantrum-throwing. He didn't like to be scolded, would say, "Mommy, you too noisy." He was immensely active and athletic—more so than either of the other two. He was happy and a good student in school, never very introspective, but thoughtful, just the same. He seemed so easy and his growing so "normal" and predictable somehow. A story that we heard years later will give you an idea what he was—and is—like. He had a group of high-school buddies who were together a lot and called themselves the Pi guys. Right after high-school graduation they all went for a couple of weeks to a beach resort to "lose their virginity." They took a suite of rooms, would cook fancy candlelight dinners and were generally rather imaginative and very funny in their escapades. I guess he was successful, because the next thing we knew he was making open sexual jokes and comments with no apparent self-consciousness. As though that was on a par with growing a beard: one day you just did it, no fanfare or guilt.

This one has had some rough emotional times with girls. He tends to be very, very loyal and romantic, and has been hurt more than once, yet hasn't gotten callous somehow, either. He doesn't ask our advice too often, but I feel certain we would know if there was any major difficulty. He bought himself a car, has a happy job and plans eventually to go back to school. Right now he is looking for a "little woman" but he is choosy. He says he wants someone like his sister (who is rather independent), someone who is "inspired." He is a jack-of-all-trades sort; most anything he puts his hand to he does well, and he is very much closer to his father than his mother, though they enjoy each other greatly. It is sometimes hard to understand why our two boys have turned out so differently—even hard to understand that they consider each other best friends.

Our daughter has had a different sort of impact on us. We used to call her the dreamer, but now that both she and we have grown up, it is clearer to us that she is enormously insightful and thoughtful about life and people. She was a joyously happy and easy child, but went into a steady unhappy decline after about thirteen or fourteen. I think we didn't understand adolescence then as we do now, and she got the brunt of our ignorance. It is sometimes a pain to us that she has had to suffer the unhappiness resulting from our lack of knowing. She left home at seventeen—a year younger than her classmates— and started college the autumn that Kennedy was assassinated. She was of the active generation and she still reflects that social consciousness, which we resisted for many years, but, by God, she isn't so wrong. We remember those college years as one mysterious pain. She came home only when she had to (she once angrily announced that she came only because they closed the dorms), and it was a battle much of the time. She was deeply lonely and unhappy all those years. After her sophomore year away she dropped out—that probably was a big turning point for both of us. We suddenly realized that if she said she wouldn't go to college, there was no way on earth we could insist. She would simply go away and work if we objected, so we didn't. When I think back now, I cringe at the lack of support we gave her; she didn't even have a private place for herself; she slept in the family room. We still marvel at her inarticulate ability to discern her own needs, and as difficult as it was to satisfy them, she managed. She truly did need a year of her own to grow emotionally and steady herself, deciding what she really wanted out of college and in her own life. From that point on she was also financially independent of us, and we still wonder why we didn't realize earlier how controlling we had been with her.

There were still several painful years before we were able to reach her. We loved her dearly, but couldn't unravel an angry, though terribly indirect, resistance. She just seemed irresponsible and distant, uncommunicative. I am not sure we liked her very much then—loved her deeply, yes, but simply could not understand her elusiveness.

The most important turning point of all for her and for us was her therapy. She got the idea and took the financial responsibility herself, and after a while, to our surprise, began to thaw into a humorous, quite comprehensible woman. To be truthful, we ourselves have changed greatly in the last few years, but some of her feelings toward us made the difference. She once said, too, that even though the letters home from her and her brothers were addressed, Dear Mom and Dad, they were, in fact, always written to Mother. Almost more than anything from her, that knocked Dad for a loop. She wasn't being critical, just factual. We both, but especially her father, have since taken a more supportive interest in the activities of our children—trying not to be parental. By that we mean that they are responsible for themselves—at least the older two—and it is none of our business the mistakes they make in attempting things. We are available to them always for advice, support and money if we have it.

The only thing we wish is that they were geographically

closer so that we could experience them more. There are few people we know who are more enjoyable, interesting or challenging than these. We do sound like parents, don't we?

I am impressed with these parents' adjustment to the painful problems of at least two of their children. As with many families, here are parents without outstandingly obvious problems who have at least one son with really major personality problems and a daughter with a painful adolescence—more painful than average. It is not the purpose of this book to go into how children from emotionally healthy families can get into severe emotional disturbances in adolescence and young adulthood, but they definitely do, and it is often agonizing to parents not to know how the problems originated and above all not to know how to help. One thing is sure: it is the essence of late adolescence to break away from needing parents, and of young adulthood to develop and firm up a life-style truly one's own. Even the best-intentioned parents' efforts to help with advice, money or just closeness are often rejected by young people who need to work out solutions, even to very severe emotional disturbances, in their own way. In my experience, those parents who can see that even the serious problems belong to the children themselves and must be solved by them are the ones who survive the best. Parents who take the blame for these problems and proceed to mastermind the solutions tend to be drawn into battles around these issues and frequently to make things worse. The most helpful attitude I know was expressed by a mother whose twenty-two-year-old daughter had a two-year depression:

It's really hard not to step in and push her to this doctor or the hospital. But she gets angrier when I do that. I've learned I must let her decide what to do. I just hold myself available to assist her if and when she wants. I don't know which is worse—her problems, or the feeling that she still needs her mama at twenty-two. I can't help

*with the problems, so at least I can avoid making her too
dependent.*

There's a fine line here, of course, and often it's impossible to walk it faultlessly. When an adolescent or young
adult is actually psychotic, can't relate to reality in a way
that is not self-destructive and gets into jails and mental
hospitals, it's hard for parents to know how much help is
enough. And professionals disagree on this. One pyschi-
atrist says, "Stay out of it," while the next says, "You
should have helped sooner." So there can't be any hard-
and-fast line here to hold to. And that's often a source
of great worry to parents. When parents come to me asking, "What should we do?" I always make sure they consider the possibility that there may be nothing helpful
they can or should do. Often it turns out that a young
person's getting himself or herself out of a serious emotional bind is the first act of self-reliance and self-help
of his or her life, and sets the stage for future independence much better than any other solution could have done.
Even someone's psychosis belongs to *him* or *her,* not to
the parents.

This is the main issue raised by these parents' description of their daughter's problems and therapy. The idea
and the responsibility for therapy came from the daughter
herself. And the changes that came from therapy belonged
to her. The formula these parents have come to understand seems to me remarkably apt. Grown children *are
responsible* for themselves; the parents are *available.* The
children must be allowed to become separate people.

PART FIVE

The process of becoming separate

CHAPTER 10

Dynamics

Dan and Peter, Sally and Emily and all the young adults in this book are struggling to define themselves as individuals in the world, separate from their parents. Their need, separately experienced, to return to Mother and Father and to work out relationships with them on new terms, got me thinking and resulted in this book. Then, thinking over the families in my practice, I began to see that parents have just as deep a need to maintain emotional contact with their children. As the interviews in chapter 9 make clear, some can imagine it only on the old terms: power in the hands of parents, and children recognizing their authority. But others can and do revise their style of dealing with their grown-up children. This is made possible because they are able to reinvest their own energy in life, giving less to "parenting" and more to careers, revitalizing their marriages, new activities and further *self*-definition. As much as the children, now grown up, need to see themselves as self-motivated and not dominated, so do parents need to retire from the parenting career and rediscover themselves as people apart from the parent role.

Twenty years ago, when I was first enthralled by Erik Erikson's way of looking at the human life cycle, I was mainly interested in adolescence. As my patients, and I, got older, I began to see how young adulthood takes off from adolescence and consolidates its changes. To get the full picture, it is necessary to look back at the earlier phases of the human life cycle and see how they set the stage for the issues of young adulthood. For me, Erikson's terms are the most fitting. What follows now is expressed in his language. One could say it in Freudian, Jungian, Laingian terms, of course. This will be a very brief developmental synopsis. For the definitive story, read *Childhood and Society*.

From pregnancy on, the issue of the relationship of mother and infant is trust—basic trust. What the mother communicates to the baby through feeding, touching, looking and holding is the message that she, and therefore people, can love and be trusted. Any conflicts she has over the rightness of her life situation and the bearing of each child will be subtly communicated to that child, as will her reactions to the constellation of qualities and primordial traits that the child has inherited. The result of their first year or so of interaction will be the establishment of some degree of basic trust or mistrust in the infant.

As the child walks and runs, the development of this locomotive ability sets the stage for a change of emphasis in the relationship of mother and child. The issue is now the development of some internal control over behavior: toilet training, a series of doubts, "good and bad" concepts. If through love and consistency some of these rules are built into the two-year-old as a basic vocabulary of values, the infant becomes autonomous—able to get by outside of the mother's direct line of sight for longer and longer periods. Should this phase fail in its purpose, through insufficient loving contact perhaps, or inconsistent or conflicted training, an inner sense of shame and self-doubt develops in the child, a feeling of "I can't be good." This is stored away, as the child moves into the next stage, when the definition of a sexual identity—a male/female choice—gets made. Now the parents' attitudes about their own sexual roles, both unconscious *and* conscious, are communicated to the child, and the child finds itself fantasying and identifying itself with the sexual roles it experiences in operation between its parents.

At about four years old, this primordial sexual predilection gets a field trial in the Oedipus situation, through a romance with a parent, partly in fantasy, partly in flirtation. Little boys try out the lover-and-father role. Of course, in every society the particular rules and customs governing the behavior of lovers and spouses are transmitted through the parents and extended family to each child. With these phases basically worked through within the personality, the child can develop a degree of initiative leading him or her out into school and away from the need for minute-by-minute contact with parents. If the sex-role issue and sexual style within the family are fraught with conflict, guilt, prudery, or seductiveness, all these conditions will duly affect each child's basic sexual role and feelings about himself or herself as a future lover.

While I am abbreviating this story drastically, it is still clear how subtle is the process of transmission of parental values and true feelings, conscious *and* unconscious, to each child. Yet we in psychiatry are now also beginning to understand that a good deal of everyone's basic *style* of reacting to life situations is genetically determined, part of our endowment. So, grossly oversimplified, we have a situation in which each parent supplies conscious and unconscious feelings and attitudes about everything important and unimportant in life to each child, who interprets and files it all away according to his or her own genetically influenced system.

What the child psychiatrist sees regularly in early life is the godlike importance of everything parents do and say; they are the transmitters of everything. And when children find that they can't live up to parents' hopes and expectations, no matter how disturbed the parents may be, it is the children who feel at fault. Children who don't get well loved feel unlovable and unworthy. Many comments made by young adults earlier in this book offer testimony on that point. Parents are the founders and guardians of our sense of self-worth. A certificate of worthiness as a person is awarded by our parents to each of us, and by us in turn to our own children. No matter how liberated and "modern" a society is, the family is always for the child a postcognitive society in which parent figures reward and punish and teach the young how to become acceptable. In this small world the parents' rules apply; their views prevail and are quite final. (Here, I think, lies the secret of why people in totalitarian societies more often than not fail to rebel but swallow the most extreme philosophies and repressions. These societies resemble early childhood: if you don't fit into the system YOU are at fault.) By the time the child is exposed to values and ideas other than those of their parents, the parental values are well imbedded into the deepest levels of the personality.

It is in adolescence that the child must reassess himself and herself in the terms of the larger world—the expectations of school, work, peers, the popular culture. At this stage not only is it not enough to be a good boy or good girl in Mommy's and Daddy's terms, it is positively to be avoided. What counts now more and more is the *peer culture* and its values. This is how people are *now* and *now* is where we live in adolescence. "Adolescent rebellion" is the rejection of nuclear family ways and the trying out of peer styles. Much of the new stuff may later be rejected—the bearded student activist may yet end up selling auto insurance in the Midwest—but the *process* of sifting through the old values and throwing away those that don't fit is what must happen now. When an adolescent feels secure and strong enough internally to tackle the process of self-definition, it is inevitable that some important changes will be made in the values parents have taught. Work ethics, sexual styles, the holy truths about marriage and having children, all will be thought over and questioned. Throughout this process, the issue is: Can I define my own values, defying my old parent-gods and still remain on good terms with them? Or will I lose their love and support if I choose to live in ways they can't approve of? In short, can I give up my parents as gods but keep them as people?

So we see people in their late teens and early twenties going home again to seek a *new* kind of validation from parents. Even as they become more separate, they are still anxious to keep the love, the closeness, the rootedness of an intact family. Most young adults, however, will not do this at the cost of their own individuality. So the task is to define and explain his or her individual life-style and choices to parents, clearly and with honest feeling. The task for parents is to hear and see the developing separateness of their grown child, and to *respect* that separateness while reserving the right to disagree with some of his or her ideas and choices. If these encounters are successful, some of the old feeling of closeness and belonging can be kept, and the family will still feel like family.

This process of becoming separate and having one's integrity recognized and understood by parents often proceeds in phases. Some of them have been documented in the preceding chapters. The common sequence is:

Step One—Young adult: declaration of separateness

This may take the form of an indictment of parents or provocative behavior which expresses: "I am not *your* creature anymore. I have feelings and values and goals different from yours, even opposed to yours!" Sally's letters, Henry's angry confrontation, Peter's cautious interviews with his parents, Melissa's talks with her parents after writing the indictment letters she didn't mail, the opening statement by the woman in chapter 7, announcing her new life-style after her divorce, and many, many examples from chapter 8 are just such opening moves, declarations of separateness.

It must be understood that phases of emotional development are links in a chain; they interlock. Even while one phase is nearing its conclusion, the next is already in process. The declaration: "I am separate from you, my parents!" must be made somehow even when there are no major differences of life-style and values to fight out. Sometimes, as we have seen in many of our interviews, the issue of life-style and value differences is kept in the forefront of the declaration of separateness, because this issue is clearer to the young adult than is the underlying need to be acknowledged as a person autonomous from the parents and regarded by them as a mature adult. When the more surface issues of "How *I* want to live versus how *you* [my parents] want to live" are stressed, parents tend to see only these issues and fail to recognize the need of their young adult child for respect and recognition as an autonomous person.

Confusion often comes from *both* sides. When a young adult has suffered severe problems in the earliest phases of childhood development, there may remain very severe conflicts over becoming separate and free from parental support. After all, when you give up your parents as your gods and judges, you must give them up as your caretakers as well. And if you are to find self-respect as captain of your own ship, you can't feel comfortable on an allowance from Daddy. In our society (not every society) we insist that our children take care of themselves financially before we can think of them as genuine adults. So at this time the resolution of the earliest stages of development is put to the test: basic trust and autonomy, versus basic mistrust and shame and doubt of oneself.

In one family I know, the primal issues of basic mistrust and self-doubt, reflecting the failure of the early relationship between a mother and her daughter, surfaced in the daughter's personality during late adolescence. Things could have been worked out at that point if the conflicts were acknowledged and talked out. But they were not. Once a good student and a creative artist, she began to fail in a particular way: she simply found herself unable to break off her need for her parents' support, while quarreling with their every belief and value in life. To her they are "materialistic, work-oriented, pleasureless, comfort-loving, not aware of the poverty and misery in the world—middle-class parasites who live off the work of the poor, without any concept of nature and ecology." All the time this barrage of shots arrives in letters and phone calls, the daughter is away at an art school in Paris, supported there by her parents. Her worried and weary father declares: "What a bind to be in! If I quit paying for her school, I feel guilty as a father. If I pay for it, I feel tricked and used. I get back no love, no respect, no gratitude, and she doesn't even do her schoolwork! After all, if I weren't all the things she hates, how could I send her to college at all?" The screw turned even tighter when he found that she had not even enrolled regularly in this school, had attended few classes and had cashed in her return air ticket, thus putting him in the position of paying for another one if he wanted to see her again.

This daughter needs to face the fact that she is trying to become free from her parents while she still feels much too needy and insecure inside herself to make a real break. If she were able to declare and implement a genuine separateness, she could later accept financial help from her father if she needed it, but as an adult. Accepting this help would then no longer require her to feel internally like a parasite, shameful. If her parents are parasites as she says, then who is she, condemning them for living off others while herself accepting their support? Here, as usual, the conflict over separation has appeared when it is due. But this young woman, in her early twenties, is still internally unable to solve the central challenge of adolescence, the formation of a solid identity. What prevents a solid identity formation is the existence of still older fossils within her developmental layers—the early life failure to feel basic trust and to become autonomous.

At the other end of the developmental spectrum, sometimes a young adult's declaration of "I am a separate person" reflects a *real* readiness to be a separate person. This moment marks the end of adolescence, as I think of it. Beyond this moment there lie ahead some vital *adult* developmental phases to be confronted: how to find successful intimacy with a particular and mutually chosen loved person, or else to face isolation; how to *generate* or produce from within oneself something that will mark one's existence in the world, perhaps children, a profession or calling, works of art, an achievement that says: "I have been here and left something of myself in the world. I have produced and added something to the world."

For the genuinely strong young adult, there are pangs over giving up dependency and parental support, but the issue is not in real doubt. The declaration "I am separate" is real and parents can sense it. As one young adult said earlier in this book, "You stop *asking* your parents for things, and you begin *telling* them what you will do." Young people look first and foremost at their parents' own solutions of the developmental issues they themselves must confront next in life. How have parents dealt with intimacy? Is their relationship really close and sustaining for both of them? Did love and caring continue to flower, or was it lost in the concerns over work, money, property, the children's needs or whatever? And as in adolescence, young adults still tend to turn to parent-surrogate figures to provide alternative solutions. If parents' intimacy seems dead or insufficient, there are other couples whose relationships can be held up as proof that intimacy *can* be preserved, that loving closeness is really more than "a passing yearning in the belly leading to entrapment in the legal, financial and parental binds called marriage." Like it or not, parents and all older friends will be considered as case examples in this quest, as young adults seek ways to meet the challenge in their need to develop further.

According to Erikson, after the developmental phase leading to the finding of intimacy (versus isolation) is dealt with early in adult life, the next developmental task one faces is "generativity versus stagnation." And again the young person, from adolescence on, looks first at what parents have generated in their lives. Are their products valuable, their works meaningful both to them and to the world? In fact, at the very moment when our adolescent and young adult children are examining our products and productions preparatory to making their own investments in work and family and art, most of us in the middle of life are asking the same questions. Has this all been worth it? *This* family, *this* marriage, *this* career, *this* way of living? If we keep our own questioning too secret, in order "not to upset the children," we run the risk of encountering their shock and rage when and if the structures we have created fall apart suddenly and without warning. Parents' disillusionment and despair are hard for children to take, but presenting them with images of perfection is very risky indeed.

Finally, the key question the young adult asks elders is the same one they ask themselves: "Has it been worth it?" What is implied in the declaration of separateness is the further declaration: "Now that I am a separate individual and an adult, I will be doing something with my life comparable to what *you* have done, or maybe I will be trying hard to *avoid* doing what you have done because I see that you are not enriched by what you have generated." It is very common these days to hear this indictment of parents from the lips of young people. And it is not unheard of for parents to encourage their young adult children's dependence upon them in order to avoid this indictment, to reinforce the structure of their own life, to justify their solutions to the problems of intimacy and generativity. A last-ditch effort is made to keep the family together (on the surface) because the making of the family was "the last thing we did together that felt good!" This is one of the deep reasons for the tremendous threat many parents feel when their childern declare themselves separate. One middle-aged mother said, "With my last child finally gone, what am I left with? My memories, what I have *really* got with my husband, and what I do with my days."

Step Two—Parents: acceptance of separateness

This means acceptance of the fact that a real message is being received, taking the message seriously and offering cooperation in negotiating the issues. Sometimes by simply offering time and space to the young adult for reflection and decision-making, as in chapter 8 (interview 4), or talking over issues in depth without judging or condemning (interview 5), parents can communicate respect for the young adult's need to grapple with these issues in a serious way, without changing their own beliefs. Listening does not presuppose agreeing.

Parents who have met their own developmental challenges successfully can handle those of their children more effectively. If you know you have a sustaining love in your life and that what you have generated is good, you don't experience your children's separation as a loss, but the passing of a phase, leaving you to enjoy them now as equals and to get on with the intimacy and generativity of your own life. You already have what they are seeking, so why begrudge it to them?

What tends to come out now is the extent to which parents *need* their adult children. Parents who can let their kids separate without bitterness are usually more fulfilled, independent people. Sometimes not, though—I have been impressed at times by parents who have been in deep trouble just at the time when their grown children wanted to become separate, and have gone along with it, getting their own needs met elsewhere rather than holding onto their children. This is an act of genuine giving.

The father in chapter 9, interview 3, faced this problem. He leaned too hard on his adolescent daughter when his wife died, and came to regret it later. "It has left her with . . . an unquenchable longing for she doesn't know what." What he did to her then amounted to a rejection of her need to be separate, overruling her need with his own (temporary) need for emotional support and help in his bereavement. This leads us to a discussion of what happens when parents *can't* accept their children's need to separate from them.

Alternate Step Two—Parents: rejection of separateness

As in chapter 8 (interviews 3, 6 or 7), parents can simply fail to see that the real issue is one of separation and becoming an individual, and become seduced into battles over the issue itself: dropping out of school, getting married or whatever. At the worst, the parents' reaction is, "You *can't* do that! We won't permit it!" This is usually when they discover the ineffectiveness of prohibition as a strategy once the child is past the middle teens. A prohibition at this stage, or refusal to listen and discuss, often provokes a further escalation by the young adult.

What are the choices for the young adults placed in this position by parents' prohibition or condemnation of what they want to do in their lives?

Not so fashionable anymore is the possibility of yielding—backing down as far as the parents can tell, letting the situation appear to ease. This choice carries the penalty of hidden rage and hurt—a loss of self-esteem, the burning self-accusation of weakness and cowardice. Whenever the next confrontation comes, the young adult who has backed down before will be angrier and more likely to go to extremes to prove he or she can't be stopped again.

Another possibility is to escalate the struggle in turn to a still riskier position—"If you don't let me do this or that, if you can't accept my plans for my life, I'll leave you for good!" And, indeed, long separations have come from this choice of action.

The most impressive course of action I have seen is unusual, because it requires maturity, a solid inner sense of one's own worth, and a decisiveness rare among young adults. This course is listening to the parental prohibition, keeping one's cool and going forward in one's own direction without rancor or retaliation. I have seen this happen particularly when the young adult has advocates or counselors available—older friends, other relatives, often a trusted therapist. These people, not emotionally involved in the young adult's life decisions, having no stake in the outcome of his or her choices, can say essentially, "What you do is up to you. Do what feels right—what matters is holding firm on the path that feels right to you."

This advice is of tremendous value to anyone in crisis at any time. How often have you received it? If you ever have, you are not likely to forget it. It is of special value at this moment in a young adult's life because his or her inner need is to declare adulthood by achieving autonomy. At this moment, when the colony no longer wants to be ruled by the mother country, the concession of common-wealth status is not enough. Separate and equal—separate *means* equal.

Step Three—Young adult: escalation

In this situation, which arises only if parents do not accept the declaration of separateness, we are in real danger. The young adults' move is often destructive or self-destructive: they are forced into a position where they must express, "No, you *can't* control me—I *will* be my-self!" To dramatize this cry, actions may be taken that are not going to work out well—as in chapter 8, interviews 3 and 7, the unsuccessful early marriage, or interview 6, in which the son rejects his mother for good.

At this point, it may still not be too late for parents to see that the situation is serious, and to change tactics. The stakes are high. If there can't be rapport now, the whole future relationship of parents and child may be negligible or attenuated and shallow. This is a great loss to all, and sets the stage for future loneliness for parents when they are old and need emotional support from their adult chil-dren. If they haven't shown respect for their children's individuality, they are less likely to get what they need from them later on. Many lonely and rejected parents have set the stage for their own isolation in this way. One way the whole interaction can be reconsidered, even after some painful attacks and counterattacks, is to find a referee—perhaps a therapist who can help with a few fam-ily therapy sessions—to show each side what the other is trying to say, and to show each what they are really saying. In situations where important family members have conflicting feelings, therapy may be the only way that offers hope. When a mother is possessive but giving double messages (like mine) or when the child is too frightened of losing security (like Billy) to make decisions and an-nounce them clearly, therapy can make all the difference.

I have seen it work that way, saving family cohesion by allowing individual development and self-expression. What all parties must see beneath the moves and countermoves in these family struggles is that in our culture every one of us *must* become separate and make that separateness clear to our parents. Parents must see and respect this, and give clear messages that they do. If this exchange fails, it fractures the family. This is, in fact, one of the main reasons why families in our society are breaking down and failing to nurture and support their members. With traditions on the wane, technology and mobility increasing, the extended family becoming just a memory among the middle class, the nuclear family is hard put to retain any meaning. Only by recognizing each member's separateness and individuality can the family make it at all.

The cultural factor is no small issue now. Under the impact of huge quantities of commercially motivating, false-to-life input through TV and other mass media, children are seeing all kinds of real and fantasied life-style alternatives to their parents' ways of living. This "information" may have been cooked up in an ad agency in Los Angeles and paid for by a deodorant manufacturer, but it is presented in the media as "real," and such data becomes part of the life-style library in children's heads. Parents have never had such competition in getting their messages across. We read that in Red China the government replaces the family in the indoctrination and motivation of youth; the dutiful son has become a Red Guard. But in this country our adolescents are remotivated by the mass media, presenting a bewildering panoply of artificial models in TV, movies and magazines, purporting to represent real life-style choices. For better or worse, adolescents are experimenting with new styles of being, challenging all the basic ways of their parents' experience. This makes it much harder for parents to respect their separateness; so much of what adolescents and young adults say and do is strange and frightening to parents these days. But, by the same token, it is all the more vital that parents should hang in and try to understand the process of development. You don't have to *agree* with your children in order not to fail them.

This is why parents must see the process of becoming a separate individual as a *normative* event of early adulthood in our culture. As adolescence focuses upon the development of a sense of identity, young adulthood must test-drive that identity and employ it in the service of a life-style that works. The process often proceeds through the phases described in this chapter; it should be seen as normal for our society at this time. This is very hard for some parents because it is not the way things were done when they were growing up. Some of the racial subgroups making up the American population have very strong traditions of extended family interdependence; one generation ago, these people decided things on the basis of what was good for the *family*, not for themselves. Parents who have shaped their lives this way have a hard time understanding the *selfishness* of the new values. Suddenly "selfish" is no longer a criticism, but something to be proud of in the minds of the young.

I recall one of the first psychiatric patients I saw when I worked in a mental hospital in Hawaii twenty years ago. A Chinese man in his fifties had suffered an emotional breakdown—he was psychotic and suicidal. The precipitating event was a controversy with his father, a man in his eighties, over a decision regarding the patient's own wife. Forced into the conflict between autonomy and respect for his father's authority, the patient broke down. The change in American attitudes over the question, "For whom do you live your life?" has been very pronounced in the past generation. So when parents face their young adult children, it is often a confrontation between people who live for others and people who want to live for themselves.

But then how can parents use their greater life experience to help their children without interfering with their separateness and integrity? What if your life experiences might help your children not to make the same mistakes you once made, and to avoid the consequences you suffered? Parents could take some counsel from a twenty-four-year-old woman I talked to. She had just returned from Christmas at home with her mother, stepfather, and her sisters and brother. She felt bitter, depressed. "It was not that anything terrible happened. It was just that we all shut down, my sister and brother and me, when we're near our parents. We're so afraid that if we show our feelings and questions, we'll get pushed or scolded as we used to do when we raised real questions that involved differences in our views and goals from our parents'!

"But I don't want to shut down at home, I want to open up. I want the experience of my mother and grandma. Now that I'm a woman and I've lost some lovers, I want to hear how Mom and Grandma felt when it happened to *them*. Now we've got adult issues in common, I want to *share* them!"

Needing *sharing,* she fears being *pushed* and *scolded.* So she "shuts down" and gives and gets nothing. What she needed was to hear her mother's and grandmother's adventures in life and love, *without* judging. More on this in the next chapter.

CHAPTER 11

Techniques

This chapter shows specific ways in which the process described in the whole book can be made smoother and more successful. One way to use it would be to check out the moves and principles outlined in it against any and all of the things the real parents and their young adult children did and said throughout the book. The other obvious way is to check and see whether one or another of these protagonists sounds like you. How did you handle these issues in your own life? You might find out you are able to modify your style in some ways that might help you with the outcome of the separation–individuation issue as it applies to your own parents, your own children or both.

To begin with, we are all in this together. To return to Erikson's ideas of what our adult lives are all about, we are trying to love and share our lives, we are trying to produce and leave behind us something of value, and if we can meet these challenges unflinchingly, we may find ego integrity as we grow old—a sense that life has been worthwhile overall, a feeling of the "rightness" or "suchness" of life. Young adults must meet the very same developmental challenges their parents have faced, and in a more complex and disturbed world. Few people that young adults ever encounter are centered and secure. Few older people seem to them to radiate ego integrity, young adults complain.

Look at it another way. The psychologist Abraham Maslow pointed out that once we have what we need for survival and physical health, we are internally driven to satisfy our emotional needs—for love, respect, belonging, sharing. And after all the battles to meet *these* needs, we find ourselves confronting still *higher* questions in the later years of our lives, like, What is important? Why do we live? We *need* to grapple with these questions, to seek answers. Our young adult children are moving up the same ladder of ever more complex human needs that we ourselves have been ascending. By refusing them autonomy or making its price too high, we are delaying their climb toward confrontation of the higher questions in life. By *being there* for our grown children, being there to listen to their life issues and to share with them our own stories and conclusions, we are furthering their growth toward maturity, even when we don't agree with the specific steps they want to take in life.

It helps a lot when you can empathize with your children or your parents; that is, the better you understand *yourself,* the better you can recognize the signs and symptoms in others of feelings you have experienced yourself. Among the jargon of the hip young, there are a couple of phrases I find really expressive. One is "to have been in that place." Often parents, when they are unusually self-aware, can recognize that once they were in "that place" where their children now find themselves. Being emotionally *available* to your child springs easiest from having been emotionally available to yourself—*knowing* yourself, or as young people say, "knowing who you are." When you know who you are emotionally, you are much nearer to knowing who your children are. And you are likely to be struck by your deep genetic/emotional resemblances. Assured of your deep human alikeness, you can then respect their separateness.

Maslow's writings on self-actualization are also very pertinent here. At every phase of life we must, we *will* encounter the challenges and problems endemic to just that particular point in the human life cycle we have reached. At every level of the mountain, there are particular problems facing the climber. To meet these challenges and transcend them is the task of each of us, and those who face the issues squarely have the greatest chance of becoming self-actualized. Every developmental issue faced and dealt with results in a leap in confidence, self-esteem and, more than that, an approach to living life as a peak experience, with a calm, intuitive sureness and full participation. Living this way, "there are . . . no near misses, only full hits." I believe that Maslow's "self-actualization" is the same as Erikson's "ego integrity"—being centered, in tune with your development.

We can help our parents and our children draw closer to this fullness of being at whatever stage they have reached. To do it, we must use our own lives as their example, demonstrating our own integrity and honesty (or lack of them) in dealing with the issues life confronts us with at the level we have reached. Our ways of working, playing, creating, loving, marrying, divorcing, fighting, being sick, staying well, understanding, giving, receiving and dying are seen and studied by our children and our parents. Children are in the habit of using parents' lives as examples, but it can and often does work the other way as well. Kevin and Sandra, at their wedding (chapter 9, interview 1), offered themselves in just this way.

Being there for someone you love is harder than hiding yourself—much harder. Listening is hard, too—we all think we do it, but if you heard yourself on a tape recording "listening" to your child trying to deal with a life crisis, you might realize, as many parents have in family therapy, that you are not really listening while your child speaks, but busy formulating your own replies. Beyond listening, you can offer your *real* feelings, in depth, about your present and past life issues, with little or no censorship. When you have failed, the data about your failure are valuable to someone trying not to fail. In medicine, we study the failed cases as well as the successful ones.

Techniques for parents

1. Watching and listening

When your young adult child expresses a direction that he or she wants to take, particularly if it is a radical-sounding one compared to your own values, *watch and listen* for possible underlying motives and needs. For example: A seventeen-year-old girl declares, "Harry and I are getting married!" If you jump in on the pros and cons of the teen-age marriage, you might miss the more vital question: What does she really want from a marriage—is there something she needs that she feels she can get only by getting married? Ask her what she's trying to find, what does she want from life, from marriage? This represents *listening* to the *internal* message contained in behavior. Maybe she'll say, as the seventeen-year-old girl in chapter 8, interview 7, did; "I'm sick of being the oldest child of six, the reliable baby-sitter and dishwasher of the family!" This can and *should* lead to some open considerations as to whether she is getting enough freedom and play and to consider who and what she wants to be, before she gets swallowed up in the wife-and-mother game.

The same would apply to the twenty-three-year-old man who announces he is dropping out of medical school. It is so tempting for a father to be shocked and to remind him of the huge investment of energy and money that has gotten him that far, and might be "thrown away" if he drops out. He might simply need a year's rest from the overpowering grind and responsibility. So the first wise move is to set up where and when the family can talk, listen to each other, hear what it's all about.

2. Don't judge

If you are going to lecture your young adult child about responsibility and not hurting your parents ("How could you do this to us," "You know your mother is nervous," and so forth), you'll surely shut off all communication. Realize that there's a difference between *feeling* and *judging*. That is, you *can* say, "Your attitude makes me angry, jealous, sad," and so forth, usually without alienating your child further, but saying, "You fool, you don't know what you're doing, you're out of your mind," and so forth, will surely end all communication and precipitate an escalating battle. A good rule for style is to talk about how you *feel*, start your sentences with, "I feel," rather than with accusations beginning with "you": "You always were foolish, you're killing me, drawing my blood," and so forth. These accusations often arouse overt antagonism and inner guilt. A young person who feels inwardly guilty is *more* likely to punish himself or herself by doing self-destructive things, *not* less.

What parents must now remember is that even though a successful encounter, recognizing the new autonomy and integrity of your young adult child will preserve closeness and friendship between the two generations, this same encounter, successful or unsuccessful, marks the end of the old *power* relationship between you. Once and for all now, the power you always had over the life decisions of this child is ended. The young adult who has declared himself or herself ready for a separate and *self*-determined life will no longer accept the old parental arsenal of weapons:

Prohibition: "No, you may not . . ."

Boycott: "We will prevent you from being able to do that . . . we won't pay for it."

Refusal to listen: "We won't hear of it . . ."

Invoking guilt: "What you want to do is WRONG!!!" "You're killing your mother . . ." "Dad will have another heart attack . . ."

Total denial of what is going on: "Never mind that, let's just go shopping!"

A power move is the wrong policy at this time, though it may have kept the children in line when they were younger. This is a time for sharing ideas and feelings, not pressure. The message is, "This is *your* life— We have suggestions or opinions, but the decisions are yours, and we will continue to love you whatever you do!"

3. *Suggest, don't command*

We *command* slaves and servants and pets; if you command your young adult child, you are bypassing his or her own independence and decision-making ability. This will often bring on an angry refusal, rather than cooperation with your goals. If you force apparent submission to your will, the seething rage will remain underneath, bound to surface later.

Suggestions, on the other hand, imply the ability of the child to hear, weigh and accept or reject the suggestions. This reinforces his or her sense that you understand the need for separateness and individuality. If the purpose of his or her initial statement or indictment or proposal was partly or entirely to demonstrate separateness, you will have shown that you understand and respect it. Thus you are already in considerable rapport. One of my favorite response styles with my own grown-up kids is: "Your idea makes me feel worried, scared or whatever. I'd suggest this or that alternative—of course, it's up to you." Then I leave it alone, unless I don't know why my son wants to do whatever it is. If I don't know, I ask, "Tell me what you want to accomplish by this." And then I listen to the *whole story*, not just long enough to formulate my objections.

4. *Be explicit as to what attitude you will take toward your child's course of action, and why*

I'll help you, I'll leave it to you or I'll try to stop you, and *why*. If you're clear at this point, your child won't misunderstand and later feel betrayed.

At this point a special word about a particular style used by some parents with their children. This is the sequence in which, for instance, a father explodes in outrage over the son's plans, refuses any help, then later becomes consumed with guilt lest the child interpret his angry outburst as meaning he doesn't love his child. This parent then goes along with the plan he earlier denounced. Now it's the *parent* who feels inwardly coerced by his own guilt and anger, and the child feels guilty over this power he has over his parent. "If Dad disapproves of what I'm doing, why is he helping me? But I need his help, so I'll use him." This combination leads to an emotional tangle and neurotic interdependence which is very hard to break.

5. No matter what, don't break off communication
It's never too late to listen. No matter how far things seem to have gone, reconnection is possible if you are willing to listen and speak your mind. There are at least three instances of "better late than never" communication and rapport in chapter 8.

Techniques for young adults

1. Watching and listening
Most of your parents' policies and moves will be in character for them, and thus not shocking to you. But bear in mind that your ideas and moves may come from values and beliefs that are new and strange to them. So don't expect them to understand and accept whatever you want to do, just because they love you. You are much more likely to shock *them,* so be prepared to explain your motives and goals. Then *listen* to their reactions.

This will sometimes be hard for you, especially if you are announcing a radical decision: denouncing marriage, deciding never to have children, declaring you are going to live as a homosexual or going on welfare. Your parents will inevitably be upset over decisions like these, which to you may represent life-style choices, but to them may suggest serious pathology in your personality or your soul. You can help them understand by letting them react with their feelings, then sticking around long enough to go into some discussion of the feelings and beliefs that underlie your decisions. Talking it all out may not bring overt understanding or agreement *now,* but you may find later that your parents have thought over what you said, and can be more understanding (even supportive) after they've had time to think it over.

Even when you are not presenting your separateness in the form of some radical life-style decision, don't assume that your parents can't understand until you've given them a chance. Their greater life experience makes them able to suggest all kinds of ways you can implement your decisions, or ways to overcome some of the problems and obstacles you'll encounter.

If your parents are uncommunicative, urge them to share their feelings with you. Help them get started in pouring out their reactions to your course of action. Just as for them, it's important for *you* to remember that the *process* of communication is just as important in the long run as the *content* of the dialogue. As one young adult said after a long conversation with his parents over dropping out of law school: "I don't even remember what we said, but it felt wonderful to be talking honestly together!"

2. Don't judge
Don't judge your parents out of hand as old and ignorant, or out of touch with life. They do have a lot more life experience than you, some of which might be relevant to your situation. Hearing them out can't hurt you. If you feel they are judging or outranking you, let them know: "When you say that, I feel judged or coerced," and so on. If they can't seem to stop judging you, suggest a neutral referee, a friend, a relative or a family therapist to do some crisis counseling.

3. Listen to suggestions, and make it clear to your parents that you hope they'll listen to yours
No matter how vexing your parents' suggestions may be, listen to them. Some of them might be very useful, and you do want them to feel they have a way to remain useful to you, to show their love and concern. Suggestions can't hurt. As in Kevin's and Sandra's wedding ceremony (chapter 9, interview 1), offer your own help and availability to

your parents in their times of need. Strong bonds of love can be built this way. If parents are to give up being authorities to you, they need to see an alternative role; *friend* is a good one, and friends do feel free to listen and advise *each* other.

4. Make it clear what action you will take, and ask specifically for what you want

To minimize confusion and feelings of betrayal, state what your decisions and intentions are. In future discussions these statements make useful points for referral. One young adult said it well earlier in this book: "For 'May I?' substitute, 'I will.' When I am firm and explicit with my parents, they are likely to accept my decisions." And that's the name of the game.

A final principle for parents *and* grown children

1. Admit it when you see you were wrong

This is much more than a homily. People who can admit their errors can be trusted. They don't have to stick to an erroneous point of view just to be right. So many people earlier in this book, particularly children, came to feel that communication in their families was eternally hopeless because parents and children were polarized into rigid postures of opposition on all important issues. Then you have to succeed in order to prove you were right, and that's precarious.

A few words about family therapy in this situation. Over the last few years, I have seen a number of families who were deadlocked in this situation—the young adult had declared firm intentions to live as a separate individual, the parents had predicted disaster. The young adult insisted, even escalated the issue by threatening disappearance from all contact with the parents; the parents had counterattacked by calling the child "disturbed," and by threatening removal of all emotional and financial help. In one case a Jewish father had said the prayer for the dead for his son, who wanted to declare his individuality by marrying a Gentile girl. At this juncture everybody in such situations is so angry and defensive that they simply can't hear what each other is saying without suspecting each other of lying and manipulating. Now a referee, someone familiar with human development, can sometimes break the deadlock by pointing out what lies beneath the surface issue. The young bridegroom-to-be may not have known that his rage with his parents comes more because they are outranking him, thwarting his individuality, than because they don't approve of his bride. He may not have understood how much he needed his parents' *permission* to be a man who makes his own decisions in life. He may also have been unaware how afraid he is of making a terrible mistake and facing the "I told you so's"—if *that* happens, will he *ever* dare to be free?

The parents may not have known that they are afraid their son does not love and respect them, and that they are outranking him now in order to hold him and his love. Yet they are doing something that is certain to lose his love. Instead of ultimatums, they need to express their love for him, their fear he is making an error, their fears that he does not love and appreciate *them* because he is violating their religious beliefs, and their fears of loss and future loneliness without him. They are using power when they want love. And power never wins love.

These parents need help to express their deeper feelings more directly, and their son needs the same. A good family therapist knows where each family member stands in his or her development and path toward self-actualization. The wise therapist knows that when any of us sees where we truly stand, we can deal with others more lovingly. We can live more fully when we're self-aware, and thus we can *let* live more fully. So the wise family therapist helps everyone see where he or she stands and what he or she really wants to say. From this point, everyone makes his or her own decisions from the heart. Unlike a judge, the therapist helps cast light upon the emotional forces in any situation, then lets the participants, now more self-aware, sort out their own decisions. By doing this, the therapist is a model for parents—and the young adult will also be a parent soon. There has been no experience in my lifework so gratifying as to help a family overcome this kind of deadlock, and to watch each member pick up once again the path of his or her own development.

To all participants

You probably *won't* convince each other of anything important. If your decision was wrong, *life* will show you that, *not* your parents or your children. As one mother and daughter, looking back, agreed:

No one ever won *any of our arguments. We just kept asking things and replying, and fifteen years later, after lots of yelling and tears, we live very differently. Now we are friends.*

The Author

SHEPARD GINANDES, M.D., has led an extraordinary career as psychiatrist, professional folk singer, sculptor, yoga teacher, professor of psychiatry and director of a "creative therapy" school in Concord, Massachusetts, known as The School We Have. While still in his teens, he cut his first records. He received his M.D. at the Harvard Medical School, where he was Instructor of Psychiatry from 1957 to 1960. Dr. Ginandes has taught adolescent psychiatry at the Boston University School of Medicine, and is presently Clinical Professor of Psychotherapy at Lesley College Graduate School of Education (Expressive Therapies Program). For the past fifteen years, his professional career has been devoted to working with adolescents: as Director of Court Clinics in Cambridge and Roxbury, as chief of a mental health team assigned to the Hawaii Youth Correctional Program and as Chief Psychiatric Consultant, Massachusetts Department of Youth Service. Dr. Ginandes is the author of *The School We Have,* a book describing the philosophy and day-to-day methods of his unique school. Dr. Ginandes is the father of four grown sons.